MW00397048

UNLOCK CREATIVITY

Opening a World of Imagination with Your Students

JACIE MASLYK

Get ready to
unlockCreativity
for every learner!

Jaci Maslyk

EduMatch Publishing

Copyright © 2019 by Jacie Maslyk

Published by EduMatch®
PO Box 150324, Alexandria, VA 22315
www.edumatchpublishing.com

All rights reserved. No portion of this book may be reproduced in any form without permission from the publisher, except as permitted by U.S. copyright law. For permissions contact sarah@edumatch.org.

These books are available at special discounts when purchased in quantities of 10 or more for use as premiums, promotions fundraising, and educational use. For inquiries and details, contact the publisher: sarah@edumatch.org.

ISBN: 978-1-970133-32-5

*This book is dedicated to all the creative educators out there--the risk-takers, the "I have this crazy idea" people, and the disrupters. Unlock Creativity exists because you are brave enough to take a chance on learning **with** your students.*

Thank you to Mandy and Sarah for your ongoing encouragement and friendship. It means the world to me to work with such amazingly smart and dedicated women.

Thanks to the entire EduMatch family for being such a supportive and connected group. Your positive energy lifts me up every day.

CONTENTS

INTRODUCTION

 Creativity is intelligence having fun. — Albert Einstein

When I was a teenager, I lived in a 100-year old brick house on a cobblestone city block. My bedroom was in the third-floor attic. I loved having the room to myself most of the time, but when my friends came over, we regularly gathered up in the attic. It was a uniquely shaped space with awkward slanting ceilings and small nooks. One evening with not much to do, two friends and I started drawing pictures on one section of a wall with some markers. At first, it was a flower, a swirly design, and then a doodle with our initials.

A few days later, my mom ventured upstairs and noticed the walls. I held my breath, waiting to get yelled at. Instead, she complimented me on the artwork and gave me the go-ahead to continue. In a variety of bright colors, my friends and I added phrases and more pictures, our high school logo, and abstract designs.

Soon one wall became two and then the ceiling. A blank canvas exploded into bright colors and bold graphics. Two years. Four years of ideas, stories, and images. The artistic graffiti became a tradition for anyone who visited our house to come in and add something to my wall. Clouds on the ceiling, a rainbow over the doorway, the sketches of friends and neighbors filled the once-empty space. It became a timeline of sorts, with pictures and words telling the story of my high school years.

The wall grew and grew for many years after that, evolving with new colors, new stories, and new wonderings. Just this year (some 25 years later) my mom finally decided to paint the walls. She had fostered the creativity in my friends and me by giving us permission to do something unconventional. The drawings had faded a bit as did the memories, but the wall served as a personal opportunity to unlock creativity. What if my mom had said no?

No, we don't have time to devote to your creative outlet.

No, we can't possibly allow this type of expression on the walls of our home.

No, you can't do that.

What if she had put limits on my opportunity to create? Do we do this in our classrooms? Do we limit the possibilities for creativity and imagination in student learning? I think at times, the answer may be yes. For several different reasons, we have limited creativity in our classrooms. In a society that is calling for innovative thinking and has a future that is quite unknown, we can no longer push creativity aside. Let's release the untapped creativity in our classrooms by fueling curiosity and embracing the imagination of our students!

CREATIVITY IN OUR SCHOOLS

Embracing creativity and innovation in schools allows for unlimited learning opportunities for students. No doubt, you have felt this recent shift in education. We have neglected creativity for some time, but now are moving away from the accountability era and into the innovation age. This is an exciting time as students are designing, collaborating, and creating in the classroom. The inclusion of innovative learning spaces and the use of technology to enhance creativity are quickly changing the landscape in our schools.

Unlocking creativity in our classrooms can lead students on a path to the unimaginable careers of the future. When we engage a learner's imagination, we begin to unlock their potential for creative thinking and problem-solving. As classrooms develop a culture that embraces creativity, innovation is possible! When we open up possibilities in the classroom, new learning can result in unthinkable imagination and incredible innovation in our schools.

WHAT EXACTLY IS CREATIVITY?

Creativity is one of those words that probably means something slightly different for everyone. It's subjective. It's not always well-defined. Creativity doesn't fit into a pre-made package.

Creativity is . . .

- noticing
- doing
- designing
- discovery
- building
- tinkering
- passion
- imagination

Creativity is unconventional and unpredictable. It breaks boundaries. Creativity is messy. So why are we doing it? Creativity opens our minds to different perspectives. It brings joy and broadens our horizons. It ignites the imagination and fuels the soul. Creativity is more than painting or dance or writing. It often expands beyond what we even thought was possible. It's the will to put your ideas out there in unique ways to explore and share with others.

Creativity happens through our wondering, exploring, tinkering, and doing. It involves playing around with ideas. It is the opportunity to take what is circling around in our imagination and bring it to life. We can foster this in our classrooms in small ways that will elicit positive change, increase creative confidence, and unlock new opportunities for students.

A CREATIVITY CRISIS

There is some question about whether we are in the midst of a creativity crisis. As a result of years of focus on accountability, have we drained the creativity out of our schools? Out of our teachers? Out of our students? Creativity is exactly what schools have been missing over the last decade or two, as assessment and accountability were the prominent themes. It is a much-needed shift to lift up our imaginative inventors, our budding artists, our skilled musicians, and our inspired architects. It is a shift that all of our students need—the ones who have incredible ideas inside their heads that they just can't wait to get out.

In a summary of *The Creativity Crisis* (Kim, 2011), the author suggests that in the late 1900s and early 2000s, education depended on lecture and plowing through textbooks and workbooks. Little opportunity was provided for projects, discussion, or collaboration. Preparation for high-stakes tests often taking precedence over quality instruction stifled risk-taking (for students and teachers) during this time.

During this time, educational systems created a fear of failure with the ongoing communication that excelling on high-stakes tests was critical. In turn, we may have a generation of students who lack the willingness to take risks and little recognition that failure is a part of the learning process. This can be problematic, as failure is essential to creativity!

Is this crisis happening because we have narrowed the scope and minds of the students we serve? I'll admit it. I've been guilty of this. In my previous role as an elementary school principal, I felt pressure for my school to achieve high test scores. We did well, but always needed to do better. I recommended reducing time on social studies and science. We devoted all of our instructional time to English Language Arts and Math (the subjects that are tested in my state). We moved away from fostering creativity and towards a serious focus on standards and test preparation. I was in the same boat as many educators and leaders who feel that pressure to achieve. Maybe we haven't limited the scope for students, but perhaps just for ourselves?

This changed for me when I started spending more time with our students, sitting down next to them as they worked or chatting with them at recess. I watched them as they prepared for a musical performance or sketched in their art classes. I observed their joy when they were experimenting in science class or building a model in social studies. I saw the passion in their eyes and the pride they felt when they created something meaningful with their hands. By reconnecting with kids, I was able to see how important this was. How could I limit them from unleashing their creative potential?

It was then that I shifted my personal focus and started looking for ways to incorporate more creativity into our school. I took the lead and gave permission for us all to step back from test-mode, take a deep breath, and look more closely at what really mattered—our students. When other schools reduced art and music classes, we increased ours. When conversations zeroed in on academic achievement, I shared the successes that we had with an approach that infused STEAM and Maker Education and championed creativity. I advocated for ways to embed creativity into our existing curriculum and tap into the imaginations of our students. I now spend much of my time passionately writing and speaking about the importance of hands-on, minds-on learning and our responsibility to ignite student creativity in schools. I feel strongly about this mission and hope that you will be implored to join in this creative journey.

WHY UNLOCK CREATIVITY?

When you were studying to become a teacher, do you remember the courses you took? They were likely general content courses that prepared you to be an elementary teacher or more content-specific if you have a specialized degree. Do you remember any classes that focused on your creativity or bringing the creativity out of your students?

Depending on where and when you went to school, I'm guessing the answer is probably no. This is part of why teaching in the 21st century is challenging. We weren't taught how to facilitate creativity in the classroom. We didn't learn how to promote innovative thinking or design in our undergraduate education. Maybe we weren't even encouraged to infuse creativity into our lessons at all. Since we are now teaching in the ever-changing innovation age, we might need a little direction for how to make that happen.

KEYS TO CREATIVITY

The four keys present opportunities for educators to unlock creativity in the classroom. These keys are by no means the only way to spark creative minds, but they will serve as common threads as we move throughout this creative journey together. Each key provides a pathway to creativity, including curiosity, choice, collaboration, and connections. The ideas shared in each chapter of this book will be linked to one or more of these Cs, the keys to unlocking creative thinking and imagination in the classroom.

Curiosity

The first key is curiosity. When we allow students to chase their curiosities, they begin to wonder and discover new things. New learning can lead to creative expression and new-found interests. With curricular constraints and assessment pressures, it can be challenging to make sure students have the time and space to do this. Be intentional about using curiosity in the classroom through discovery learning, questioning, and reflection. Throughout the chapters, you will find lesson ideas for how to generate curiosity within your students.

Choice

The next key to unlock creativity is choice. When we give students choices, we personalize learning, and students become empowered. Empowerment extends beyond engagement and offers students both options and opportunities in the classroom. This means stepping away from teacher-directed learning and towards a more student-centered approach. It doesn't just mean in our instruction, but in our classroom design, our instructional approach, and our assessment procedures.

Collaboration

Collaboration is the third key, which can be a source of creativity as students share ideas with others and feed off of the imagination of their peers. Some students may need to feel the support of a collaborative group, while others may not. Collaboration is one step toward building stronger relationships in the classroom. Provide choice when it comes to collaboration so that students can learn to work productively in a group, but also begin to understand their personal strengths and needs as a learner. Collaboration can empower a group of creative thinkers as they see their ideas build and grow through the contributions of everyone in the group. Examples in this book will include lesson ideas that can be done individually or in small groups, weaving options for collaboration throughout.

Connections

Creative connections to critical content exist, if only we take the time to explore them. Connections to student interest, connections to real-world experiences, and connections to creative experts can open up new pathways to learning for students. While some students make creative connections naturally, others may need some guidance to discover different channels to support their creativity. As educators, we spend time thinking about the way that ideas may link to one another and how we can use these links to benefit students in daily instruction.

Unlock Creativity will share small ways to foster creativity in the classroom. You will find light bulb icons throughout every chapter. These represent opportunities to develop classroom creativity through lesson ideas. Some ideas will be simple, easily implemented tomorrow, while others may take some time and resources to accomplish. The ideas apply to all ages, grades, and subjects. Also, many of the activities can be used to develop our own creativity as adults. Each chapter will end with Creative Considerations followed by Invitations to Imagination. Creative Considerations is your chance to reflect on the chapter and consider some questions to move your thinking forward. Invitations to Imagination is the opportunity to act. Here you will find ideas that can be implemented immediately. With three options, hopefully you will find one that resonates with you.

Throughout the chapters, you will also find a page out of my Creative

Notebook. These stories are shared to provide a personal connection to creativity and inspire you to reflect on your own creative journey.

If you agree that it will be creative citizens that will solve the problems of the future, then I challenge you to join me as we look at ways that we can reimagine our classrooms to unlock the creative potential of our students.

If you feel like you've lost your ability to be creative in the classroom or believe that student creativity needs a jumpstart, then this book is for you. It's for teachers who want to reimagine what teaching can look like in a creative classroom. It's for school and district leaders who recognize that students are more than test scores. It's for curriculum leaders and instructional coaches who want to rethink school curriculum by infusing creative opportunities for all learners. This book will provide tools for you as the teacher to increase your personal creativity as well as strategies to empower your students. This book is for anyone who wants to unlock creativity in powerful ways by unleashing our imaginations and create exciting possibilities for kids!

BEGIN WITH BELIEF

 Every child is an artist. The problem is how to remain an artist once we grow up. — Pablo Picasso

TRAIN FOR CREATIVE AGILITY

Our mind may be our most powerful tool. It empowers us as we build personal confidence. It gives us the courage to pursue new interests and drives us to accomplish things that we never thought possible.

Think about the focus and commitment of those who run marathons. Runners are able to successfully complete marathons because they dedicate their time to preparation, to developing themselves physically and mentally. Before they begin to set up a training schedule, change their diet, or wake up early in the morning to run, they take that first step. They allow their mind to believe that their body can achieve the challenge in front of them.

It is because of this belief that marathon runners look beyond this and picture themselves crossing the finish line. While it may be many months down the road, they envision their success. They may experi-

ᴊoubt during the process. Only when they solidify the belief that ᴊshing the marathon is possible, then they are able to push through tremendous obstacles and find success.

Being a creative person is very similar to being a marathon runner. When we believe that we can be creative, we take the first step toward creativity. When we take a moment to visualize the finish line, we are preparing ourselves to look past the doubts that try to dissuade us. It is only when we believe in ourselves that we can unlock creativity for others.

Educators will need to believe that they can build creative agility in themselves, and then take steps to achieve it so that others can learn from their example. With schools stepping away from creativity in the classroom in recent years, educators will need to build creative agility in themselves. You wouldn't go outside tomorrow and decide that you're going to run a marathon if you haven't run in a while. Building your physical skills is similar to building your creative skills. Each step in practicing those skills improves your stamina and agility. When we build up creative agility, we are taking small steps towards a larger goal, building our muscles and strengthening our creative core, which happens through brainstorming, refining ideas, reflecting, and adjusting.

When you build capacity and develop creative agility in the classroom, it can be applied to anything you do. Creativity can enhance our ability to solve problems, work as a team, and function in a global society. We can all build our creative muscles and become more agile by being intentional about embedding creativity into our daily practices both in and out of the classroom. Let's take some small step towards increasing our own creativity and the creativity of our students.

You are creative. You were born to run.

> ## WHEN WE BEGIN WITH THE BELIEF THAT WE CAN DO IT, WE CAN ACCOMPLISH ANY TASK.

THE COURAGE TO LEAD

In order to begin with belief, we need to generate some creative confidence in ourselves and have the courage to lead creativity in the classroom. This means taking a risk as the lead learner and taking a courageous leap into something outside of your comfort zone. We need to model this creative courage for our students by showing them the ways we express our creativity and flex our creative muscles in the classroom.

Some may say, "I'm not creative. I'm horrible at drawing. I certainly can't carry a tune." That's ok. We all have something; we just need to take the time to uncover it. Some creative ability that may spark an interest in our students. Some skill or interesting talent that can model for students that creativity comes in all shapes, sizes, and colors. Find the courage to believe in your own creativity. It's in you, but something may be holding you back. Don't let fear, uncertainty, or some other barrier get in your way of believing that you can complete your marathon.

Our schools are often the creative centers of our communities. It's where we showcase student talent and imagination through art shows, musical concerts, and creative exhibitions. In every classroom, there e a future Picasso, DaVinci, Jobs, or Disney. The potential lies in students that walk through our doors each day. There are future designers, engineers, inventors, and makers right in front of us. We have to be vulnerable in the classroom and show students that building our creative agility can lead to amazing things so that they, too, will find the courage to express themselves in creative ways.

When we possess the courage to try unconventional methods of instruction, this can lead to a spark of creative learning for our students. Let's be willing to dedicate time to developing our students and ourselves as creative, imaginative individuals. These are our creative exercises as we prepare for the marathon. Believe you have what it takes to unlock creativity in the classroom so you can muster up the courage to run that race.

BUILD CREATIVE STAMINA

Just as runners work to prolong and sustain their physical efforts, creative thinkers need to take similar steps to push our minds to generate ideas and develop our creativity. Beginning with the belief that we can do it is the first step in accomplishing any creative task. We need to practice our creative habits—try new skills that will keep our creative muscles building and our minds stretching. This ongoing exercise builds our internal belief in our own abilities and also equips us to help develop stamina in others. Increasing our stamina means extending the time that we spend focused on creative tasks and increasing our ability to pursue creative ideas and processes. We must help build the courage to take creative risks in our students as a part of our own stamina building.

Our creative stamina allows us to generate new ideas and bounce them off of existing ideas. It incorporates our ability to try new materials, develop new routines, and engage in new types of learning. Those with creative stamina are looking for ways to activate and sustain creative momentum through the development of creative habits. They are always looking for an imaginative twist, their thoughts brimming with new possibilities and wonderings. If this doesn't describe you, don't worry. This book provides a variety of simple strategies you can use to develop your creativity by adding small steps to your daily routine. Together, we will build our creative endurance, adding stamina and agility to our skillset as creative thinkers in the classroom.

CREATIVITY NOTEBOOK

My friends and colleagues know that I carry around a notebook with me, just about everywhere I go. My philosophy is, you never know when you might encounter a bright idea or new inspiration.

This notebook is a means for me to jot down things that I don't want to forget or capture thoughts or images that resonate with me.

Sometimes my notes connect to something that I am currently working on and other times I look back at them after many months and rekindle the idea.

While the notebook may be a traditional tool in this digital age, I love the feeling of the pen against the paper, scribbling out a word, or drawing lines to connect one light bulb moment to another. Doodles, to-do lists or pages full of text, my notebook collects my creative (or not so creative) thoughts and keeps them in a place that I can revisit and reflect on.

INCREASE OUR CREATIVE STRENGTHS

If we want to unlock creativity in our classrooms, not only do we need to build up our creative stamina, but we also need to train for creative agility. Creativity may come naturally to some, but for others, creativity may require a roadmap to model creative thinking. Recognizing that you may not consider yourself to be creative yet, there are some habits that can help you to not only believe in your potential creative genius, but also in the ability to build your own personal creative agility.

Creative people demonstrate traits that extend beyond having skills in art, music, writing, or architecture, although those are undoubtedly creative pathways. Here are some daily practices of creative people:

- Gather lots of ideas.
- Reflect often.
- Try new things.
- Be interested in different cultures.
- Seek out connections between different ideas.
- Appreciate feedback.
- Ask questions.
- Consider different perspectives.
- Share personal journeys (including mistakes).

These practices are the foundation for creative thinkers. They keep our minds engaged and our creative muscles flexing. Once we commit to building our own creative abilities, we can take steps to build our creative muscles in simple ways.

DEVELOP A PERSONAL PLAN

Just as marathon runners map out their training plan well in advance of their race, creative thinkers may need a plan too. These athletes increase their running times each day and design their meals for optimal performance for many months in preparation. Similarly, you can prepare for your creative journey by developing a personal plan for creativity.

Step 1: Choose an item from the list above or from the personal list that you created. For example, gather lots of ideas.

Step 2: Focus on one idea that you will intentionally model for your students. Establishing creative habits doesn't happen overnight, but you can build them through creative "strength training" over time. Try one idea for the next week. This will help to develop your creative agility. As you model one creative habit, bring it to the attention of your students. There is power in letting them know that you are a learner working on a new skill.

Gathering lots of ideas may be something that you do in a journal or maybe through a video diary. You might stop during class to write down a new idea in your journal. Modeling for students that you are building your own creative habits will give them the chance to believe that they can do the same.

Step 3: Develop your portfolio of creative habits. Show your students that you are learning and growing in your creative process and progressing in the plan you've developed. Here are some ideas you might want to try as you build your creative agility.

- Draw your to-do list.
- Make a paper airplane.
- Take a timeout (2-3 minutes of quiet).
- Do a jigsaw puzzle.
- Plant a flower.
- Handwrite a note or a postcard to a friend.
- Try a physical activity from childhood (hopscotch, jump rope, jacks, hula hoops).
- Take some photos of colorful images around you.
- Mess with some Play-Doh.
- Sketch your favorite place to visit.
- Take a nature walk.
- Start an "I Wish" journal.
- Create a mind map of your favorite movie, book, or song.

When we create a personal plan, we are committing to the belief that we can develop our creativity. Pausing to engage in these tasks may prompt your personal reflection but may also propel you into other creative tasks. Adding thoughtful reflection to your creative plan will demonstrate the importance of writing and thinking as a creative learner.

We are adding to our exercise regimen a practice that will build our skills as teachers and as learners, and we are stepping out of our comfort zones to demonstrate our creative courage by trying new strategies. Our students may be inspired by the steps we take, which can encourage them to strengthen their creativity as well.

REFLECT ON PERSONAL CREATIVITY

Belief in your personal creativity comes from within. Think back to your childhood. What memories do you have of making, creating, or building? What are those joyful moments? What images come to mind? When you sit and reflect on that, are you flooded with creative memories? Building forts in the woods, finger painting, creating with Play-Doh. Maybe you tried your hand at latch hook rugs or built structures with Tinker Toys. When we reflect on our own experiences, we will likely find those moments of creative inspiration.

A few years ago, I came across an article about the Maker Movement by Gary Stager, one of the authors of *Invent to Learn*. His work has really stuck with me, so much so that I always share one particular quote whenever I talk with educators. Stager says,

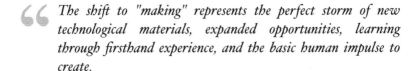

> *The shift to "making" represents the perfect storm of new technological materials, expanded opportunities, learning through firsthand experience, and the basic human impulse to create.*

Think about the ways you fulfill your basic human impulse to create.

Some educators are quick to come up with their creative outlet — the way they act on this innate need to express themselves in creative ways. For others, they puzzle over what they personally do to unlock their own creativity. Some say, "I don't think I do anything creative." Part of this may be because they really don't engage in creative habits, but it is more likely that they just don't believe what they are already doing is creative enough. Jot down your impulse to create here:

HUMAN IMPULSE TO CREATE

_____

_____

_____

_____

_____

_____

_____

_____

_____

There is real power when we share our stories with others. Take the time to share your personal story with your students. Share the joy of childhood creativity and be an example for students that creativity is rewarding and memorable. To take this step toward unlocking your creativity, try this simple Reflect and Respond strategy, and see where it takes you.

Reflect and Respond is an opportunity for you to recall your personal memories and your abilities as a creator in a way that can model creativity for your students. Here's how it works:

- Write down an idea or sketch a picture of your personal impulse to create as a child. You might even create a timeline of creative memories.
- Next, respond to that same question now as an adult. What's your creative outlet? Do you garden or enjoy woodworking?

Do you sew or build models? Do you cook or write music? Reflect on your human impulse to create and jot down your ideas.

- Now reflect on your childhood creativity compared to your current creativity. Do you carry on your childhood creative impulse as an adult? How have your interests changed? Do you think you are more or less creative? How does that carry over into your educational practices?

Tell your students stories about your childhood creativity. Share with them what you do as an adult to fulfill your impulse to create. Maybe your students are interested in painting or gardening just like you! Not only will this build all-important relationships with your students, but it will allow them to see another side of you, a creative side that can provide inspiration to students looking to pursue their own creative passions.

PLAN CONVERSATIONS TO INSTILL BELIEF

As you build your own creative muscles, add new creative habits, and reflect on your personal experiences, begin to think about sharing your story with others by looking for opportunities to have creative conversations. The more you talk about creativity and share your habits with others, it may deepen your belief in yourself. Creative Conversations are one simple way to unlock creativity in the classroom.

Have the courage to share your creative stories with students. Maybe you've given sewing a try (and failed miserably). Or perhaps you have a thriving garden at home and could share some pictures with your students. They may find inspiration through your personal examples. To get started with this process, share about a time when you:

- accomplished a creative task that seemed impossible.
- created something with a family member.
- experimented with something colorful.

- watched a YouTube video to learn how to fix something.
- made your own music.
- built something out of nothing.
- took a class to learn something new.
- tried something creative and failed.

Your conversations can focus on something serious such as sharing your disappointment from an unsuccessful submission to be published or a failed attempt at home remodeling. Conversations can also be humorous—like bringing in a clay pot that you made for your parents when you were seven years old.

Don't be afraid to be vulnerable with your students. Our creative efforts aren't always successful, but by sharing your experiences, you can provide an authentic example for your students. The more we share, the more we are reminded of and believe in our own personal creativity.

Reflect on how you might extend this creative conversation with your students. Here are a few ways you can use this strategy:

- Plan a creative chat during your morning meeting with students:
- Did anyone try something creative this weekend?
- Who wants to share a creative wondering with the group?
- Turn it into a writing prompt:
- Write about a time when you tried something new and failed
- Share what you believe to be your biggest creative accomplishment
- Encourage students to bring in an artifact from home that someone in their family created (Think: a picture, a blanket, or even a food item):
- Share it by creating a display of creative artifacts within the classroom or doing a "show and tell" (no matter what grade level you teach!)

Be intentional about infusing creative conversations into your classroom this week. These conversations will demonstrate your personal belief in yourself as a creative individual, but more importantly, it will show students that they have creativity inside themselves. It will also allow students to see your creative side, as well as the vulnerability that it takes to build creative stamina.

EXERCISE YOUR CREATIVITY

If we are going to lead creativity in the classroom, we need to try some activities that will get our creative juices flowing. Jump-starting our own creativity through simple tasks can build our own creative agility and get our minds generating creative thoughts. Start building stamina with short, no-fuss tasks that can help educators reflect on their own ability to lead creative conversations.

In *Creative Confidence*, the founders of IDEO share stories of creative design happening in corporations and schools across the globe. In one chapter, they explain the 30-circle challenge (Use the template in the Appendix or create your own.) On an 8 ½ x 11" sheet of paper, in 6 rows of 5, there are 30 hollow circles. The creative challenge is this: fill the circles with something different in each. With what you might ask? With anything. With whatever comes to mind. In whatever creative fashion works for you.

This task can be used as a quick creative activity, taking only two to three minutes. Provide a variety of writing materials from pencils to Mr. Sketch markers. You'll find that participants will draw pictures like smiley faces or objects that fit nicely into the circles. Others connect the circles turning them into body segments of a caterpillar or wheels on a bicycle. When time is up, ask the group to share. There are often sighs of relief when the self-declared "not creative" individuals see that their ideas are similar to their peers.

The task is meant to show that everyone can be creative. The flexibility of the activity makes it applicable in different contexts and can work for learners of all ages. Here's how you might use it in your classroom:

- Icebreaker at the beginning of a new year:
- 30 circles that are all about you (hobbies, family, friends, inspirational quotes or anything that represents you as an individual)
- Brainstorming tool:
- generate as many possible solutions as you can to a problem (math)
- jot down as many symbols as you can that remind you of the environment (science)
- sketch 30 things that were invented before you were born (history)
- list as many traits to describe the main character in a story (ELA)
- Brain break activity:
- create a 30-image gallery of your favorite emojis
- sketch 30 reasons why your classroom/school is great

This quick challenge is one way to jumpstart creative thinking and build the belief that you can take a blank page and turn it into something whimsical. The open-ended nature of the task promotes creative thinking and can be a way to initiate conversations in the classroom. Activities like these can help to build creative agility in our learners and show them that their creative ideas are worth sharing.

BUILD CREATIVE CONFIDENCE

Now that we understand the importance of believing in our creative abilities, we need to engage in building our creative agility and stamina. Building our skills and training our muscles will equip us to serve our students. Creativity is more than music and the arts. It is more than painting and poetry. Sure, it can include those things, but creativity is the spark of belief inside of all of us that must be nurtured and developed. Creativity can no longer lay dormant in schools. It needs to be poked and prodded and unleashed so that we can maximize student learning—and it starts with you.

We don't have to be amazing artists or designers to lead creativity in our schools. Small ideas can unlock creativity for teachers and students. Embed tasks with a creative flair throughout your content and give students the opportunity to build their creative agility within a safe and nurturing classroom environment. If we can model creativity for our students by developing our own creative habits, there are no limits to our learning.

CREATIVE CONSIDERATIONS

When we begin with a belief in our creative abilities, we will find there are opportunities to create all around us. As teachers and educational leaders, we are training for a creative marathon because this work begins with us. Building our creative agility through new habits and routines will help us to strengthen our muscles for that big run. We can take steps to model creativity and extend invitations to our students to create. Creativity is within all of us! Reflect on these three questions to help deepen your creative belief and growth.

• How do you model creativity and show students that we all have a creative spark?
• What stories can you use to initiate creative conversations in the classroom?
• What creative habits are a part of your personal routine, and how might you share this with others?

INVITATIONS TO IMAGINATION

Practice building your creative skills and build belief in yourself. It's not always easy to be vulnerable in the classroom. The following three actions can help you to build stamina and agility to unlock creativity. Unleash one action this week and commit to believing in your own creativity.
• Create an opportunity to create with your students.
• Foster your creative stamina and adopt one new creative habit this week.
• To build creative agility, plan one small task that can provide open-ended opportunities for creation like the 30 Circle challenge. Take a photo of your 30 Circle activity and share it with the #UnlockCreativity community.

EXPLORE THE UNKNOWN

 Our job is not to prepare students for something. Our job is to help students prepare themselves for anything! — A.J. Juliani

THE IMPORTANCE OF TAKING A CHANCE

Some of the greatest innovations begin with a creative individual sharing their ideas with the world. Apple founder, Steve Jobs, is thought to be one of the most innovative people of our time. He was willing to take a chance on the unknown and explore innovations in technology that many people had only dreamed about. He brought new ideas to life that have changed our ability to connect, communicate, and get information.

The next Steve Jobs may be sitting in our classroom today, just waiting for the chance to unleash their ideas. The deciding factor between a student who demonstrates creativity and one who fears to let it out may be you. Be the teacher who encourages creativity and finds the spark within each student that will bring about innovation. Without taking the time to allow the creative side of his mind to explore, Steve Jobs would never have been able to design, build, and create.

Inside all of our classrooms, we have creative potential that can be unleashed when we design opportunities for students to use their imaginations. Exploring new instructional approaches and exposing learners to unconventional materials are ways we can build creativity in the classroom. Exploring the unknown may also mean taking the chance and letting students be decision-makers in the classroom. Unlocking opportunities in the classroom means holding students at the heart of everything we do.

Only when we embrace our own creativity, demonstrate it in our lessons, and dare to face the fears we have regarding it, will we truly encourage our students to do the same. The hunger to explore the unknown lives in all of us and is at the forefront of our creative minds. Embrace it and your students will as well.

EXPLORING IMAGINATION

In order to delve into the unknown, we have to let our imaginations run free. Stretching our minds beyond what we have always done in the past and thinking about how to refocus on creative strategies may take us into new territory. As educators, we have to be willing to let go of tradition and explore the many ways that we can expose our students to different facets of learning. At times, this may mean veering from a planned lesson or being uncomfortable as we learn about something new.

For students, the unknown represents possibilities. The possibility of new learning can engage creative students and pull in those who may not yet hold the belief that they have creative strengths. We want all students to develop critical thinking skills and activate their minds in new and interesting ways. That can't happen if we don't model what it means to explore the unknown and take risks. When we fall back on providing instruction in the same exact way we have in the past, without tweaking or improving it, we are missing an opportunity for personal growth. When we don't grow, in turn, we may hinder the growth potential of our students.

Our students deserve the opportunity to activate their imaginations and engage in experiences that will prepare them for life beyond our classroom walls. As students are encouraged to imagine in the classroom, they will explore their creative abilities and begin to build the stamina that it takes to strengthen their creative agility.

CREATIVITY NOTEBOOK

In the classroom, it can be a challenge to think about where creativity "fits in". It can't be something extra that we add on or that we only do for a special lesson.

I remember being a first grade teacher and thinking that if I had an art corner, then my students would just start creating stuff. What I quickly realized was that they didn't know how to get started. I had to model the creative process for them at first. I had to show them that finger painting was messy and that origami was tough!

My students enjoyed the opportunity, but they still viewed it as separate. I had to rethink how I was designing my lessons and looking for ways to embed creative opportunities into the work we were already doing.

Start by asking students, "how will you show me that you understand this (lesson, unit, concept)? Let them share the ways that they can infuse creativity into the learning. You never know what they'll come up with!

MAKE LEARNING RELEVANT

Exploring the unknown can be scary, even intimidating, but it is important to understand that this type of learning is relevant for our students. When we provide learners with a problem that has an unknown solution or with open-ended challenges that can result in all sorts of unique responses, we are pushing them to think about what is possible. This type of thinking is becoming increasingly important as the jobs of the future will require flexible, creative thinkers.

Relevant learning experiences are those that our students will use now and in the future. Learning that is relevant connects to student interests and aspirations. The way that we design these experiences is critical to the creative development of our students. We can foster personal relevance for students by listening to their interests and offering choices in the classroom that connect to our learners. The content that is relevant to our students may be new and unfamiliar to us, but this exploration is critical to unlocking their creative minds.

Relevant learning for your students may mean exploring ideas like STEM or STEAM education or the use of maker learning in the classroom. The reason why these strategies have increased in popularity over the last 10 years might be because of the integrated approach to content. In classrooms where STEAM is embraced, it is through the interconnected nature of the subject areas that students begin to see the relevance in their learning.

Connecting ideas in STEAM means that robotics can connect with literature and that art is present throughout science. It means that engineering can be enhanced through the use of technology and that any combination of these subjects creates a more meaningful learning experience for students than exploring single subject learning on its own. This provides a relevant and imaginative pathway for students. The interconnectedness of subjects mirrors the work that students will engage in beyond their school experience, so it is critical that we design these types of opportunities for our students. These relevant educational practices provide students with problem-solving and teamwork skills that are necessary for college, career, and beyond.

STRATEGIES FOR DISCOVERY

Venturing into uncharted territory can be frightening, and the less we know about something, the more fearful of it we become. The people that make the greatest difference in our world, however, are the ones who are brave enough to take a step toward the unknown to further themselves and others. Our most creative ideas will sometimes lie on the other side of fear and may require the use of unorthodox methods or materials to see them through.

So how do we step into the unknown and explore relevant, imaginative learning in the classroom? The following ideas will help you to spark the imagination of your students. The key is to provide exposure to strategies and materials that instill the belief that all students are creative when they are given the opportunity.

> **UNLOCKING OPPORTUNITIES IN THE CLASSROOM MEANS HOLDING STUDENTS AT THE HEART OF EVERYTHING WE DO.**

DISCOVER NEW LEARNING MATERIALS

Every creative thought begins somewhere. For some people, it may come through something they have seen or experienced. For others, it may require a more tactile approach. Helping to build creative agility within our students can be fostered through the materials we provide and the learning experiences we design. Unconventional learning materials in the classroom lead to unconventional thinking on the part of our students.

Getting ready for science class? Set out springs, rocks, or magnifying glasses. By including relevant materials to tinker with, we can stir up the minds of our students to engage them physically in the learning. Prepping for math class? Share Lego bricks, dice, or a measuring tape. These manipulatives might help students to connect with the content while also providing hands-on options within the lesson. Starting a poetry lesson? Give students clay, beads, or nuts and bolts. As students listen to poetry, they can mold and mess with different materials which provide tactile learners with a chance to engage their senses and also let their minds begin to wonder about the possible learning connections. Create your list of potential materials below:

UNCONVENTIONAL MATERIALS

_____

_____

_____

_____

_____

_____

_____

_____

Different materials can inspire students to create their own poetry or build the patterns that they hear within the text. Having these materials available can help your students who may need to focus but will also help your creative thinkers to keep their minds moving with new ideas. Here is one way you can utilize unconventional learning materials in the classroom:

- Create a tinkering space or an area where students are free to access and use materials in different ways. This might include found or purchased materials that provide a more tactile experience for students while also providing a potential spark for student creativity. Dedicate a table in the classroom or simply a bin where students can explore with new materials.
- This might be something students do when they walk into the classroom as a warm-up or an idea generator within the context of a lesson. Having materials accessible to students helps them to see the possibilities in the items around them, but also engages them in the creative process within the context of their classroom lessons.

- Consider making your tinkering space a learning center that students could visit at certain times of the day. Taking brain breaks to tinker with new materials can unlock creativity but also allow students to refocus when they return to academic tasks after having time to play with materials.

This will look different in every classroom, depending on the grade level or subject area that you teach. Consider the types of materials that might engage your students.

- Learning about plants and seeds? Include an invitation to tinker with a tray in the middle of the table with seed pods, leaves, acorns, and flower petals. Students can explore the items within the lesson as a springboard for creativity. When students interact with the materials, they are learning to explore on their own while furthering their understanding far more than if they were just to read about them on a page.
- Is your class reading about the five senses? What items might you include for each sense? Brainstorm a list that might include textured materials like sandpaper, felt, satin, or burlap. Consider materials that create sound or incorporate smell like bubble wrap or dryer sheets. The hands-on nature of the exploration may spark creative writing, drawing, or inventing.
- Empty out your junk drawer! Everyone has one. As I peeked inside my drawer at home, I found a playing card, some stickers, a plastic Easter egg, colored paper clips, and some plastic straws. These and other random items could be used to generate creative ideas or even new inventions through hands-on tinkering.
- Use loose materials from a tinker tray to create something: a pattern, a collage, a self-portrait, your name. As students explore with loose materials, there are creative possibilities that extend beyond any models we can provide. Students will connect ideas together as they connect materials. Exploration through tinkering allows students to make their thinking visible through the use of simple materials.

The open opportunity to explore materials can be a springboard for creative ideas. If you're not sure what will meet the creative needs of your students, just ask them. Pose a question on the board or put a suggestion box in the classroom and ask what materials might be useful in the classroom. By asking students for their input, they will become more invested in the process and will already begin using their creative minds from the start.

In many elementary classrooms, students study the life cycle of a butterfly. Some add classroom pets in the form of caterpillars and watch how they grow and change over some time. Students love to watch this metamorphosis that culminates with the release of the newly evolved butterflies. How do you assess this? Do students take a quiz? Write in a butterfly journal? Label a diagram? These are all reasonable options, but how might we add a STEAM twist that embraces creativity? Don't limit student assignments to one format. Expose them to a variety of possibilities. When we allow students to explore learning using the pathway they enjoy the most, students are more inclined to draw on their creativity.

Picture this:

Students draw the life cycle on a piece of paper, showing the stages of egg, caterpillar, chrysalis, and butterfly (or whatever stages/terminology are appropriate to your grade level and curriculum). Then have students use Ozobots (a small, round programmable robot) and program them to physically move through each stage of this metamorphosis, demonstrating both creativity and understanding. Adding a creative layer to student learning and assessment creates opportunities for students to develop skills in multiple content areas, as opposed to just one.

Looking for a low-/no-cost way to accomplish this same task? Try the augmented reality app 3DBear https://www.3dbear.io/. Students can retell any story or process, like the metamorphosis of a caterpillar using images and text within the app. For another free tech twist, try Tynker and have students create the code to demonstrate the change from a caterpillar to a butterfly. Better yet? Offer a variety of creative tools for students to use and let them choose the one that best meets their interests.

Learning opportunities like these blur the lines between the content areas. Students are exposed to science and technology without always realizing how the two relate. When we read books about the creative intersection between math and art, and tinker with tools as we build and design, STEAM learning is in action. As educators, we can be intentional about planning integrated lessons that promote creative opportunities to think and collaborate through STEAM learning experiences.

EXPLORE STEAM THROUGH STORIES

Engaging students in STEAM learning can feel like unknown territory for some. Exploring hands-on learning with students can result in unknown outcomes as students hypothesize, experiment, build, and create. The authenticity of STEAM learning means that we can't predict the outcome of what our students will come up with. That is creativity in action!

The integration of science, technology, engineering, art, and math through STEAM education offers students the chance to connect creative ideas across subject areas. When multiple subjects merge together, student learning soars. STEAM learning can come together through engaging stories of invention and the creative characters found in picture books. Our students can creatively engage in STEAM learning using children's literature as a pathway to imagination. Creativity and design can be found within many stories, especially those that are focused on content in science, technology, engineering, art, and math.

Let's explore books and design creative opportunities for students. Stories like *Ideas All Around* by Philip C. Stead prompt student thinking and provide opportunities for students to wonder and imagine. As they read, creative thinkers explore the world around them along with the storyteller. Readers experience the process of how ideas are born and nurtured through the environment and the people we interact with. Subtle connections to science, engineering, and art are infused throughout the book.

In another book, *On a Beam of Light: A Story of Albert Einstein,* Jennifer Berne tells a story of curiosity and wonder as the young scientist pursues new knowledge leading to amazing discoveries. His passions in science allowed him to explore the relationships among light, sound, magnetism, mathematics, and motion. Einstein was playful, loved music, and had a vivid imagination. This is the type of passionate energy we want from our students. How can we help our students find inspiration in a book?

Try this:

- Choose a creative STEAM story to share with your students. Check out my website www.steam-makers.com for a full list of literature options that can provide valuable learning experiences for students.
- Think about how you will use literature to reinforce concepts in science, technology, engineering, art, and math while also encouraging creative thinking and innovative practices.
- Pair the book with a creative task like one of these:
- Recreate part of the story by building it with clay.
- Sketch a part of the story that resonated with you using physical or digital tools.
- Write about the STEAM concepts that were evident in the story, then animate them using digital tools like Scratch https://scratch.mit.edu/or stop-motion animation.

You might be asking yourself — is this just an elementary thing? While children's literature is used most often in the elementary grades, there are lots of great examples of higher-level texts that support hands-on creativity connected to content. Consider survival-themed books that provide natural connections to creativity and problem-solving through the ongoing struggles of the characters. *Lord of the Flies, Island of the Blue Dolphin, Sign of the Beaver,* and *Hatchet* are just a few examples of stories that can lead to creative STEAM learning.

Think about the possible opportunities to create that can come from these rich stories:

- Build a shelter for the characters based on the elements in the story.
- Design three tools that the characters may need in the story using natural materials.
- Create a signal that would help the characters to get rescued.
- Devise a system that will help to keep the characters safe from danger.

The outcomes of projects like these are open-ended, leaving a variety of possibilities for student learning, but that is the beauty of creative exploration. The creative integration of multiple subject areas is a part of the real-world work that students will do in the future. It can be found within picture books, poetry, and novels. When you find an opportunity for exploration within a book, extend the learning and allow students to unlock their creativity by thinking, designing, and making. What other books might be used to prompt creativity through STEAM?

STEAM STORIES

_____

_____

_____

_____

_____

_____

3 WORD DESIGN CHALLENGES

Skills for exploring the unknown can be developed through the use of design thinking in the classroom. Creating design challenges for students provides an opportunity for learners to explore with a variety of materials and use their imaginations to solve both simple and complex problems. Design challenges are learning tasks that present a problem, need, or a challenge that students need to overcome. They are provided with a variety of materials to accomplish the task and will likely have some sort of criteria that students will need to consider. Many challenges also incorporate STEAM subjects with students tapping into their knowledge of geometry, physics, and art without even realizing it.

Design challenges don't need to be complicated. When you really think about it, a lot of tasks can be boiled down into three words. That is the idea behind the 3 Word Design Challenge.

Build a bridge.

Code a robot.

Design marble mazes.

Just. Three. Words.

For example, in the challenge Two Concurrent Towers, students are given a table full of materials to build two towers of the same height. The catch is that there are no duplicates to any of the materials provided, so creating identical structures proves to be a challenge. The goal is to create the two tallest towers possible (at the same height) with the materials provided. You might share the following with students (remember, just one of each item):

- styrofoam cup
- plastic fork
- straw
- pipe cleaner
- shoebox
- pencil
- crayon
- paper plate
- rubber band

- index card
- craft stick
- aluminum foil
- any other household or craft materials

This is an open-ended challenge, but you can certainly set some limits on the challenge to put the pressure on. Try adding time limits, setting aside just two minutes to draft a plan, five minutes to build, and two minutes to share and reflect.

Looking to upgrade the challenge? After teams have worked on their designs for a few minutes, throw a wrench into things. Tell teams to select one member of their team who will go and steal an item from another team. This forces groups to rethink their designs. Another twist to add is to offer additional materials that might help the group accomplish the task. Need some duct tape? You'll have to trade in two other items in exchange. This causes teams to prioritize and think creatively about the challenge.

Here are some other three-word design challenges that can be done in any classroom:

- Build a Bridge
- Drop an Egg
- Create a Game
- Repurpose a Box
- Can it Float?
- Make it Move
- Ship a Chip
- Deconstruct a Toy
- Two Concurrent Towers

Hands-on challenges are one way to encourage collaboration and allow students to use their imagination in response to the challenge, similar to when students engage in STEAM learning or explore the unknown with tinker trays. These challenges can be used as a team-building activity at the beginning of a school year or to build collaborative capacity throughout the school year. More detail on these challenges

and others can be found on my blog Creativity in the Making https://
jaciemaslyk.blogspot.com/2018/01/3-word-design-challenges.html.
Creative challenges can be aligned to content in math and science or
connected to a piece of children's literature. They provide a pathway
for students to use their imaginations and unlock creativity in
extraordinary ways. What other three-word challenges can you come
up with?

3 WORD DESIGN CHALLENGES

_____
_____
_____
_____
_____
_____
_____
_____
_____

CREATIVE EXPLORATION

Students thrive when they can activate their imaginations in the classroom; to explore creative materials, different texts, and instructional
strategies. Start creative exploration by providing students with opportunities that are relevant to their interests and needs. Design hands-on
learning opportunities with engaging materials and open-ended challenges. We don't have to know exactly how creative learning will turn
out, but we have to take that chance. Exploring our imaginations can
have powerful outcomes for our teaching practices but also for the
creative development of our students.

CREATIVE CONSIDERATIONS

When we take a chance and explore unfamiliar approaches to learning, we are unlocking the potential for student creativity. Whether we incorporate STEAM learning experiences or introduce our students to a variety of unique learning materials, we are presenting an opportunity for students to design and create in imaginative ways.

• How might you expose students to unconventional materials within your classroom?

• How can open-ended challenges be incorporated to foster student creativity?

INVITATIONS TO IMAGINATION

Take time to explore the unknown in the classroom by adding strategies that will extend the imagination of your students. Relevant, hands-on opportunities can activate student creativity and problem-solving that will help to prepare students for an unknown future.

1. Introduce Tinker Trays into your next lesson and allow students to explore with unique materials.

2. Share your favorite STEAM-related book on social media or capture the creativity in the STEAM challenges that you try in class.

3. Design a lesson to explore familiar materials in an unfamiliar way and create your own 3 Word Challenge. Share it on social media and don't forget to use the hashtag #UnlockCreativity.

CREATIVE RESOURCES

Random Story Generator
https://random-story-generator.drhowey.com/
http://www.scholastic.com/teachers/story-starters/

Create Comics
http://www.toondoo.com/
https://www.mykidsadventures.com/create-comic-strip-kids/

Color and Paint
https://www.coloringpaintinggames.com/
http://www.tuxpaint.org/

Art Projects
https://artprojectsforkids.org/
https://babbledabbledo.com/80-easy-creative-projects-for-kids/

Make Music
http://www.nyphilkids.org/
https://www.sphero.com/specdrums

Creative Writing
https://www.journalbuddies.com/creative-writing-2/creative-writing-ideas-for-kids/
https://www.kidzone.ws/creative-writing/book-picture.htm

CHANGE THE SCENERY

 Creative environments give people time to experiment, to fail, to try again, to play, to make connections among seemingly disparate elements. — Sir Ken Robinson

INSPIRING PLACES TO LEARN

Have you ever visited a museum and become inspired by all that is surrounding you? Maybe you've visited a friend's home, and the cozy feeling compelled you to want to cook or bake. Perhaps you've traveled to the beach and felt an increased desire to eat healthier and exercise more. It's remarkable how a change in scenery can change our attitudes, our mindset, and even our level of creativity.

A walk out in the courtyard to get some fresh air. Just a few minutes in the sunshine. A quick stretch to jumpstart our workflow. It can be a small shift in our practice by changing our setting that can refocus our minds. Sometimes we might just need a little more inspiration than our current environment provides. A stop at a coffee shop or a walk to the local library. Perhaps a stroll through an art shop for some creative inspiration. As adults, we recognize our own needs as a creative learner and have the ability to change up the scenery to give our minds a much-needed adjustment. Our students need that change in environment just as much as we do.

How often do we stop and consider what a change in scenery can do for our learners?

When we change the learning environment in response to the needs of our students, we are making a commitment to their creative growth as individuals. We can change the scenery in the classroom and involve our students in that process. Whether through small shifts or larger changes, the environment that we learn and work in each day can have an impact on our ability to think, collaborate, and create.

Changing the scenery provides a change in perspective. Something different to look at, to feel or experience, and it may be just what we need. This change may be something small, like a colorful view out the window or a walk down the hall. It might mean sitting in a special seat or being able to stretch our legs. The environment we learn in may enthusiastically trigger or sadly hinder our creative mindset. The change of scenery has become a prominent topic in education recently, as classroom teachers and school leaders are reflecting on learning spaces and the way these can enhance student learning and creativity.

Consider the contrast between the rows of seats in an auditorium and the message that sends compared to the cozy, collaborative seating arrangements in a local bookstore. What we see, hear, and feel can change our level of creativity. It can stifle our imaginations or allow our ideas to soar! It can be a scenery overhaul when we adjust our environment to support creative thinking and collaboration for our learners. Within our classrooms, we can change the scenery and create an optimal environment for our learners.

CHANGE MAY MEAN RISK

Gone are the days when the teacher stood front and center in the classroom spouting their knowledge out to a group of students sitting in rows merely serving as receptors of information. This may sound a lot like our own schooling experience, but we cannot continue down that path. When we reconsider our learning environment and assess the scenery, we should include the voices of our students in the process.

When we change the scenery in our classrooms, we can look from a different perspective. Gaining a new perspective can provide a creative spark. Feeling stuck in a desk or a classroom can put constraints on our creative thinking. A change in the scenery can provide a new view that allows us to look through a new lens at a topic, a lesson, or a problem.

Educators are taking this risk by leaps and bounds. With an increase in flexible seating and the development of cozy classroom spaces, we are taking steps to create environments that not only welcome students in, but that offer spaces that meet the needs of different types of learners. Any change can feel risky, especially one that transforms your classroom environment. Think about the ways that you might begin to change the scenery in ways that will benefit your students and consider their needs and interests as learners.

GATHER PERSONAL PROFILES

OK, you are ready to make some changes in your classroom, but where do you even start? You will spend 180 days sharing the classroom space with 20-30 other people. Include them in the conversation. Even students as young as kindergarten can share their ideas with you and develop their own personal profiles for the optimal learning environment. Personal profiles could be as simple as a one-page list, a drawing, or a Google Slide. Learners could design a visual profile with a creative twist, taking photos or creating an image of themselves and incorporating details about what they prefer as a creative learner. This profile could include the conditions that benefit them most in the classroom setting. For example:

- I prefer to work when the lights are dim.
- I am more creative when the sun is shining through the windows.
- My ideas flow when I work alone.

- A small group setting helps my creative thinking.
- When the classroom is noisy, I struggle to find my creativity.
- I need a quiet space to be productive and create new ideas.
- Sitting on the floor helps me to focus on my work.
- I need a desk to feel organized and ready to work on a creative project.

What other factors might you consider? Ask your students! Create an ongoing list of characteristics that might be a part of someone's profile. Students will have many more thoughts on creating a learning environment that will work for them. Share or display these ideas in the classroom. Some students may not even recognize what they need to learn best. Opening the discussion and sharing these preferences may help bring out the voice of others. Ask students how those ideas can be incorporated within the classroom. While painting the walls pink or giving everyone their own recliner might not be manageable, take time to brainstorm ways to make it work for you and your students.

We can unlock the creative potential of our students and empower them when we include them in the creative design of our physical space. Teachers recognize both the simple and complex ways they can alter the teaching and learning environment to better meet the needs of their students. When students have choices in their learning environment, creativity can thrive.

WHEN STUDENTS KNOW THEY
ARE VALUED, THEY ARE FREE
TO THINK, CREATE, AND
DREAM.

ESTABLISH TIME AND SPACE TO CREATE

Change up the scenery by providing students with the time and space to create. Many schools are fortunate to have innovative learning spaces that encourage creativity. Sometimes these spaces are in the library, a multi-purpose room, or somewhere within the classroom. The creative learning space might even be outside. We need to ensure that learners have time to create both within our own classrooms and throughout our campus. This might come in the form of scheduling structures to promote creative activities. It could also be in the form of after-school programs or clubs. It might mean allocating flexible learning time for students to engage in creative learning.

What does flexible learning time look like in your school or classroom? Time in a makerspace provides opportunities for students to direct their own learning and uncover new knowledge. They choose the materials. They design the projects. Maker learning can be an extension of a unit that you are already teaching, or it can be a stand-alone opportunity for students to discover new ideas, to tinker with new materials, and to get messy. Incorporating maker learning into your existing curriculum means adding a layer of hands-on exploration to your content (and across content areas) and exposing students to tools and materials that will allow them to demonstrate creativity. We have to be intentional about creating time for our students to design, tinker, and make. Within our already busy school days, how can we ensure this happens?

- Establish a makerspace corner within your classroom. Check out www.steam-makers.com for makerspace ideas and resources.
- Reflect on potential outdoor learning space for students.
- Sponsor a maker club before school, after school, or during recess.
- Consider offering summer programs for students that focus on creativity.
- Use "non-teaching" times during the day to focus on creativity with students.

We can change the scenery by extending student learning at different times and in different places. How can students activate their creativity when they are at recess or other unstructured times? Chalk for the sidewalk or painter's tape on the cafeteria walls can turn into works of art. Creativity walks on the school grounds can support students who are looking to change the scenery midday. Thinking flexibly about our time within the school day may lead to new creative endeavors.

CREATIVITY NOTEBOOK

My birthday is late in August, right around back to school time. This was great when I was young because it always meant that I'd have new clothes to wear to school, but it was even better when I became a teacher because I'd get cool things for my classroom as birthday gifts. One year, my mom bought me a throne made out of heavy-duty cardboard. This thing was huge and sturdy and I could not wait to share it with my students!

As a classroom teacher, I taught kindergarten and first grade. I love that age because it is such a critical time in their literacy development. The birthday throne was the perfect addition to my classroom as our "author's chair."

The students and I painted the chair and added it to our class meeting area. As the students worked through the writing process, they would sit in the throne and read their work to their peers. This became a coveted spot where students felt empowered to read their words and share their personal writing with others.

Student confidence was built and creativity was boosted, just by adding something new to the space.

CO-CREATING LEARNING SPACES

If you are looking to change the scenery, start right there in your classroom. Create a learning space that welcomes learners in and inspires them to be creative. The flexible seating movement is taking over classrooms and libraries everywhere. Our learning spaces are being redesigned and redecorated to be more engaging environments for student learning with colorful accents and different seating options. Who better to help co-create these spaces than our students?

We have finally broken out of the model of uncomfortable desks in uniform rows with four beige walls. Does anyone really feel creative in that kind of environment? Classrooms are becoming more colorful, comfortable places where students can choose to stand at a table and work or gather on stools to collaborate with their classmates. Students can plop down on a bean bag chair or balance on a stability ball if that is more conducive to their personal learning preferences. This not only gives students a choice, but if we do flexible seating the right way, it also gives students a voice to share what kind of environment maximizes their learning. Take a step to co-create the classroom space with your students. List a few things that you might consider changing within the space.

CO-CREATING LEARNING SPACES

_____

_____

_____

_____

_____

_____

_____

_____

_____

OK, so now you have this wish list of changes that you'd like to see in your space. What are you going to do about it? We don't always have the funding to bring our ideas to fruition, so let's think creatively about solving this problem. Creating a Donors Choose project or writing a grant are certainly possibilities, but don't overlook the resources right in your own community. Reach out to your parent/teacher organization and see if they have any funding to support new ideas for your learning space. Ask a local community business to support your class by donating or buying just one item. Get your students involved and have them brainstorm ways to enhance the classroom environment.

Co-creating the learning space means just that. We are a team designing the classroom space together. If we as teachers decide to bring 25 of the same seating into the classroom space, we are not providing flexible options for students. Taking steps to change the scenery <u>with</u> your students will make the adjustments meaningful to students and create an atmosphere that supports student learning far beyond the creative tasks presented here.

One innovative teacher took a co-designing approach with her students introducing four different seating options within the classroom:

- Traditional desks with chairs
- Standing desks with a foot bar
- Low tables with cushions on the floor
- Stability balls

Each morning, the teacher asked students to choose a seat, a spot that would work well for their personal learning style. Throughout the day, she checked in with students to see how the seating was meeting their needs. She wrote down some of her personal observations about student choices, as well. At the end of the day, she asked them to reflect on whether that spot worked for them or not, so that the following day, they could make a more informed decision. Sometimes students would adjust their preferences each day, while others would stay in the same seat for weeks.

On Fridays, she would reflect with the entire class on whether one of the choices should be removed and other options circulated in. One student preferred a traditional desk, while three others were hoping they could bring in a couch. Two students preferred floor cushions, while another asked for a podium where he could stand most of the day. One group of students advocated for more stools to be brought into the classroom. They liked how the stools could be moved easily, and different groups could work together. The discussions with students led the teacher to adjust the learning environment based on their needs and preferences.

We want our classrooms to be engaging spaces where students are free to collaborate and create. Changing up the scenery based on student needs creates a positive environment for collaboration and creative thinking. The learning environment should be a welcoming place that opens up new opportunities for learners, not one that stifles their ability to collaborate, explore, and imagine. If we are going to transform our learning spaces, then we need to include the most important people in those decisions, and those are our students.

Here are a few examples of how you might co-design space and change the scenery to support student creativity:

- Organize a classroom design challenge:
- Teams of students create the blueprint for the new classroom space.
- Propose a plan for procurement for their recommended purchases (furniture, decor, etc.).
- Can we petition the parent organization for support?
- Might local businesses or organizations provide donations?
- Present their creative design to the class.
- Establish a design corner. This can be a dedicated spot stocked with art supplies, a table with a large jigsaw puzzle, a wall with a giant coloring page, block toys for building. All of these examples can be offered within your classroom as a way to tap into student creativity in informal ways. These are invitations that can be used with any grade level or subject area. Learners of all ages will enjoy being invited in to help solve a puzzle or contribute to coloring a life-size map of the world. Providing these examples around your classroom and throughout the school present opportunities for students to engage in creativity in so many ways.
- Survey students or hold a class meeting about the decorations, theme, or color schemes that should be included in the classroom. (Just because you love a chevron pattern doesn't mean they will.)

Tap into student creativity and pull them into the decision-making process when it comes to changing the scenery in the classroom space. Ensuring that your classroom provides creative inspiration is a responsibility that both you and your students can take on together. Classroom design can leverage voice and choice but also build a sense of student empowerment in the classroom.

DESIGNING ENVIRONMENTS FOR CREATIVITY

Our students have been trained to be receivers of information in school. We present the information. They consume and regurgitate it. Transferring ownership over to your students can be a challenge. Asking them to engage and create may be new and uncomfortable for many students, but we need to encourage them to think like creators, not consumers.

One way to empower students to change the scenery is through the design of the learning space. This is also a way to tap into student creativity. Students are coming to school increasingly more aware of their own learning strengths, but they often have to check those needs at the door and conform to the way school is structured.

We can partner with our students as we create learning spaces that support creative thinking and collaboration. We can include students in decision making with creative input on what we are learning about, how we will learn it, and where the learning takes place. Our students can tap into their creativity by helping to customize the design of the physical space in the classroom and changing the learning environment to foster their creativity. Each instructional shift and each decision we share with our learners represents an opportunity for students to find their voice in the classroom and make choices about their learning in both big and small ways.

CREATIVE CONSIDERATIONS

It's funny how a change in the scenery can change our perspectives. As we change the scenery, both physically and instructionally, we will need to build trust with our students and allow them to share in leading the learning within the classroom. This can unlock their creativity when they are given a chance to express themselves, make decisions, and explore their passions.

• In what ways can you change the scenery to create new opportunities for your students?

• How does your classroom environment promote creative, collaborative work?

• How might we bring students into the design process, building ownership over the classroom space?

INVITATIONS TO IMAGINATION

Changing the scenery in our classrooms provides choice and engagement for our students. Activating the creative mindsets of our students can happen when we change the environment to meet the flexible and creative needs of our students.

1. Invite students to share their learning preference by developing a learning profile using whatever creative methods they choose.

2. Share ownership in the classroom by letting students design the space, one corner, a bulletin board, or entryway. Post a picture of a classroom space that you co-created with your students using #UnlockCreativity.

EMPOWER EVERY LEARNER

    *Changing the game of school means actually allowing students to
create their own game. This is empowerment.*

    — John Spencer and A.J Juliani

VALUE STUDENT PERSPECTIVES

"I'm not sure all of the classes are going to be interested in that."

"I agree. We need to think about what the little kids are going to want too."

"What if, we moved the sewing stuff over to that corner?"

"We still need to think about where the computers will go, maybe putting two or three on that counter. We're going to need that for coding projects."

This is just a snapshot of part of a conversation with some fourth- and fifth-grade students as we planned for our makerspace to move to a new location. As the building principal, I had consulted with our maintenance and technology departments and even talked with a colleague who worked at our local museum makerspace. Our team of teachers had visited a variety of spaces to get a sense for the features we wanted to include, but it wasn't until I sat down with a group of students that I realized that we had missed the mark!

The group of students included boys and girls who had used the previous space for a few years. Some of them were really into robotics, while others preferred woodworking. Some were artistic, and others were mathematically-minded. They were open and honest about what they thought the makerspace needed. They even shared components of their grade level experiences that connected to maker learning. They were the users of the space, the makers, the architects, and the artists. They knew what would work and what wouldn't work. Why hadn't we asked them in the first place?

When we took the time to value their perspectives, we learned a lot about what making meant to them. We benefited from insight into their interests and needs in the space just by opening up the conversation. We discovered what topics and projects resonated with them and how we would move forward, responding to the needs of all learners. While we thought that we'd considered everything, there were clearly things we missed. Our students told us. We always valued their perspectives; we just make enough space to truly hear their voices.

EMBRACE YOUNG EXPERTS

As educators, we don't hold all the knowledge; we are no longer the only experts in the room. Every member of the classroom has something to contribute. Our students have the passion to pursue innovative solutions to complex global problems. They have the technological knowledge to design, code, and program in creative ways that we can't even imagine. They have the creativity to reimagine their learning space and transform it into something magical. Yet some educators continue to lead teacher-centered classrooms that limit the ability of students to be creative and provide input into the development of a shared classroom environment. Sometimes stepping out of our comfort zones and taking a small risk for the benefit of our students can lead to a larger, long-lasting impact.

When we step aside and share the classroom with our students, we are showing them that we trust them. We trust that they can make responsible choices, collaborate effectively, and lead the learning. When students get to make decisions that direct what they will learn and how they will go about learning it, we can unlock their imaginations and empower students in meaningful ways.

When we give students a voice in the classroom, it means more than just listening to them, although listening is a good first step. Student voice means that we honor the opinions, beliefs, and ideas of our students, and we find ways to use their contributions within the classroom. This might happen through feedback like voting in the classroom or using student surveys. Student voice can happen in more academic ways like classroom debates or student-led parent-teacher conferences.

Student voice can also happen in creative ways like Genius Hour or passion projects where classroom time is devoted to students choosing topics of interest, and to researching and pursuing new information about those topics. When students engage in these types of self-selected learning, they aren't limited to book reports or speeches. They can creatively choose what and how they will learn. Passion-focused projects can result in personalized learning that includes design, artwork, costumes, video, or any other number of creative ideas for students. When students are empowered to make creative choices in the classroom, the possibilities are endless.

Empowering your students to take ownership of both their learning and their learning environment is an important first step towards unlocking creativity in the classroom. Giving students the power to lead, make decisions, and drive instructional change in the classroom taps into creative genius and helps to build the trust needed to create in the classroom.

We have to be ok with taking the risk and showing students that we are vulnerable in this way as well. It shows students that they can be vulnerable too. It's not to say that students need to be included in every decision and co-create everything, but we need to look for opportunities where students can voice their opinions and needs within the classroom. Sometimes, we just need to step out of the spotlight and let it shine on our students. Students who are empowered in the classroom know their voices will be heard. When students know they are valued, they are free to think and dream.

INCORPORATE STUDENT INPUT

One key to unlocking creativity is choice. As adults, when we are given choices, we feel the flexibility to express ourselves. When we are trusted to make decisions as leaders in the classroom, our ideas flow more freely. This applies to both teachers and students. When teachers are empowered to make choices, they explore new materials and think differently about embedding creativity into their practices.

Student choice happens in similar ways. When we give students options in the classroom, we are building their capacity to think for themselves and solve problems. They are empowered when they can choose a topic to learn about and decide how they will use their learning time.

By building in opportunities for student choice, we give students the chance to think about what works best for them as a learner.

Just as you and I have learning preferences, we can work with our students so that they can recognize their own personal profile. These small factors within our classroom setting can make a difference. Let's think about how we can take steps to empower students in the classroom. Do students have a say in...

1. ...where they learn?
2. ...when they learn?
3. ...how they learn?
4. ...how they show what they know?

CREATIVITY NOTEBOOK

Student choice sounds good, but it is a real challenge. How do you give up control in the classroom and allow students to make decisions?

One small step at a time.

Some 20 years ago, as a primary grade teacher I remember being terrified to try learning centers. Would my students be able to work productively without my direct facilitation?

Yes! With the gradual release of ownership over tasks, even my 5 and 6 year old students were able to take responsibility and engage in learning independently.

When it comes to creativity, every child needs the opportunity to create on their own. It may be risky to let them choose materials. You may be afraid to see the end result of a messy project. It's OK. Your students need this. They deserve the chance to build their creative stamina and you can help them to do it!

As educators, how do we establish a culture for creativity and innovation in the classroom that puts students at the center of teaching and learning? It starts by creating opportunities for students to explore new materials and new ideas. This can be further nurtured when we allow student voices to be heard and choices in learning to be made. In turn, we can step back and share the leadership with our students.

Giving up control of the classroom can be unnerving. My goodness, who knows what will happen if we let students choose how they learn or what materials they will use. As a former elementary principal, I often spent time in our makerspace at lunch so that students could come in and tinker as a recess alternative. One day a group of students was messing around with some K'Nex, building, chatting, and making. As their ideas grew, they started looking around the room for additional materials—some cardboard, markers, and tape. They continued to work, adding a motor (part of one of the K'Nex kits) and some cardboard for a propeller. They soon realized they wanted to create more movement in their design and needed another motor and some attachments. One student suggested, "Hey, what if we use the stuff in the Snap Circuits kit to make it work?" The kids methodically combined the two kits together, mixing and matching parts. Their collaboration on this project was in sync, and their imaginations were on overdrive. What more can we want as educators?

Keep in mind, we generally tried to keep materials organized and maintained like parts and pieces in one spot. The organizer in me wanted to yell, "Step. Away. From. The. Snap. Circuits!" but the maker in me said, "Yes! Keep innovating!" The students had a vision—one that was creative and successful in their design. They knew how to accomplish their idea and worked together to make it happen. If I had interjected, it would've conveyed to the students that order and organization were more important than their creativity.

Think about how many times that happens in schools. We often intercede and try to maintain control because we are afraid of what might happen. We shouldn't make instructional decisions based on our comfort level as the teacher in the classroom. We must base decisions on what will make our learners thrive. I could've easily stifled their creativity that day and tried to control the learning, but instead, I bit my tongue and trusted that my students knew what they were doing. By supporting their creative genius, the message was clear — unconventional thinking can lead to remarkable learning for students. Are we willing to take that risk and take a chance for the students we serve?

LET STUDENTS LEAD

One way to empower students to make decisions about their own learning is to let them decide what they are learning about. We can step out of the classroom model and the traditional teaching roles to provide students with a change in the scenery. This can happen in small ways within the classroom as we encourage students to choose topics they are passionate about, or to select the novel for literature circles. It can also happen in big ways when we show students that their interests are valued when we work together to allow students to drive their own learning process. A powerful way to accomplish this is through the Edcamp model. The EdCamp Foundation https://www.edcamp.org/ has a variety of resources for you to learn more about implementing this model.

After a group of educators attended their first Edcamp, they returned invigorated about the possibility of a student-led version of Edcamp. Known as an "unconference," Edcamps are personalized learning days developed for participants by participants. With no pre-set agenda or formal presenters, Edcamp is a day-long opportunity to explore any topic that you choose. It is a model that provides self-directed, small-group learning based on interest.

Instead of teaching their scheduled classes one afternoon, the teachers set up a scheduling board in the cafeteria and created their own middle school version of the model. The set-up began as every student was given the opportunity to write down some topics they were interested in learning about. The students looked a little puzzled when they were handed sticky notes and were asked to write down any topics that they wanted to pursue. "Anything?" Yep. Anything.

It was as if the light bulbs clicked on as the students begin to generate their ideas learning how to tie-dye, create henna tattoos, or design a website. Some focused on trading football cards, while others pursued learning interesting facts about the Civil War. The topics were all over the place, but this was student voice and choice at its finest! The students spent two afternoons pursuing learning through this student-centered model. This option allowed the students to collaborate, be creative, and indulge in their curiosities. It also gave students the platform to make decisions about their learning. In EdCamp, there is the "rule of two feet." If the learning isn't meeting your personal needs, then participants are encouraged to use their two feet to walk away and find another group that works for them.

Let students lead.

These teachers let their students lead the learning. Why don't we do this more often? Is it that we forget that they can or are we too afraid to let them do it? Don't let fear prevent you from exploring a creative path that students are interested in—even if it doesn't fit into your lesson plan. Effective teachers don't let limitations detract them from their goal. They think about the ways that veering off the path can meet learning goals, push student thinking, and unlock creativity.

- Host a student-led Edcamp for the day. Check out #SLEdCamp for pictures and ideas from other student-led personalized learning days.
- Can't commit to a full day? Try an Edcamp period in your classroom. Just one class period where students can decide what they want to learn about and connect with others who want to learn, too.
- Try the EdCamp model during recess or set aside any 30-minute chunk of time to try it in your classroom.
- Partner up with another teacher or two and expand the experience for students.
- Better yet, connect with another class virtually and create a cross-country collaboration where students can learn something new together.
- Explore Genius Hour https://geniushour.com/ and devote one hour a week for students to pursue a topic that they are

passionate about. Based on Google's 20% time, Genius Hour is the idea that learners can be given one hour every week to spend pursuing knowledge that they choose. A student interested in baseball might research every baseball park in the nation and share that knowledge with the class. A student interested in fashion design might teach themselves how to sew and display their creations for their peers. This is a time for students to choose an area of study that excites them. The culmination includes some type of reflection and sharing based on the time spent on their project.

When we let our students lead the learning, they are changing the scenery within the curriculum, making choices about the way learning should look and feel. We are empowering them to actively engage as opposed to just sit and consume information presented by the teacher. We are inviting them to participate in planning instruction driven by their interests. As a result, students begin to open their minds to the possibilities of learning in creative ways about new and interesting topics. This will foster student creativity as learners are provided with the freedom to activate their voice and choice in the classroom.

CREATIVE CONSIDERATIONS

Shifting power over to our students through voice and choice is a process. This can unlock their creativity when they are given a chance to express themselves, make decisions, and explore their passions.
• What is one step that you can take to let your students lead?
• How might you create a stronger sense of student ownership within the classroom?

INVITATIONS TO IMAGINATION

Changing the scenery in our classrooms provides choice and engagement for our students. Activating the creative mindsets of our students can happen when we change the environment to meet the flexible and creative needs of our students.

1. Plan one way that students can decide on the learning. Empower them to create assessment options or plan the next learning unit.

2. Promote student leadership through making. Try maker learning in the classroom or makerspace as a way to foster student voice and choice.

MAKE TIME TO PLAY

 There is no innovation and creativity without failure. Period.
— Brené Brown

A CREATIVE MINDSET

When I was little, probably four or five years old, I remember playing with my favorite aunt. She was always creative, but in simple ways. She would make up games and find ways for us to be silly together. I remember sitting at the kitchen table and drawing pictures together while we waited for dinner to cook. We would draw one part at a time. She would draw a circle for the head, then I would draw a body, telling a story as we went along. We'd draw a little girl with long eyelashes and a bow in her hair. We would design a ruffled dress for her because she was going to a party. She would need some high heels that were usually red or pink. She'd need dangly earrings and a fancy purse. We would chat about what the girl would do at the party and who she might meet.

Sometimes, we'd draw a witch with crooked teeth and a black mole on her chin. We would laugh about what she needed to find to make her spells. By no means were we artists, but together, we created some imaginative stories through our shared drawings. My aunt was intentional about developing my creative mindset early on in life. She created opportunities to engage in creative play, imaginative thinking, and storytelling. Our carefree drawing time together helped to develop my creative mindset.

In education, we have embraced the innovator's mindset, encouraged a growth mindset, and worked to develop a maker mindset. Developing a creative mindset in the classroom can happen in several ways. Many proclaim that you can't teach creativity, but you can nurture it by developing dispositions with your students that serve as a foundation for a creative mindset. Consider where your classroom falls on these continuums:

- Curiosity or indifference?
- Flexibility or rigidity?
- Community or isolation?
- Productive struggle or comfort?
- Creativity or uniformity?

CREATIVE MAKERS MESS WITH THINGS AND AREN'T AFRAID TO GET DIRTY. IS YOUR CLASSROOM A PLACE WHERE MESSY LEARNING IS OK?

A creative mindset just doesn't happen overnight. It requires time and attention to build the character traits of creative thinkers and makers. The Maker Movement is one pathway that is bringing back play and tinkering in our schools, and it can support the development of a creative mindset for students. The hands-on nature of making also activates student voice and choice as learners find their strengths and select projects they want to work on. The development of a mindset for making doesn't just happen in a makerspace. This mindset is fostered in every creative classroom, library, and learning space.

Play through making is a must in our schools. It serves to benefit not only students, but educators, schools, and communities as we nurture the creative mindset. When our students develop a creative mindset, they begin to embrace imperfections, build a sense of community, and develop empathy for others. Making can also spark student imagination as we foster an entrepreneurial spirit. Most importantly, making nurtures a creative mindset.

We need to provide opportunities for students to find that spark and create some magic by taking steps to rethink the way we do things in the classroom. Do we carve out opportunities for our students to be imaginative thinkers or artistic designers? Do we encourage their abilities as digital dynamos, inventive engineers, or creative storytellers? Developing a creative mindset in the classroom means embracing the creative strengths of our students while also developing new ones.

What characteristics do you believe are a part of a creative mindset? Jot down a few key characteristics.

CREATIVE MINDSET

_____

_____

_____

_____

_____

Did you include things like collaboration or perseverance? While characteristics like these are often considered "soft skills," they are the foundation for a creative mindset within our students.

CREATIVITY NOTEBOOK

When I was little, I went to a Montessori school. I have lots of memories from this time despite only being three or four years old.

I remember pushing broken crayons around on a hot plate covered in wax paper and watching the colors melt together in fantastic swirls and designs.

I remember feeling special when I was responsible for preparing our daily snack, which one morning happened to be alfalfa sprouts and peanut butter.

I remember making our own books with cardboard backing covered with fabric from my grandma's sewing room and writing our own stories inside.

I remember going on nature walks and bringing back treasures like pebbles, pine cones, and oddly-shaped leaves.

This was my learning.

It felt like play, yet it built my curiosities and fueled my knowledge of the things around me. Play is learning.

POSSIBILITIES THROUGH PLAY

Our students are curious. They are playful—endlessly looking for ideas all around them. They look for the possibilities in a cardboard box. They look at a bedroom wall and see a colorful mural. Our students wonder. They observe. They are curious about the things around them, always thinking and considering new possibilities.

Creative thinkers see the possibilities in everyday objects and envision new inventions by combining things together. A creative mindset is one that is always moving, generating new ideas and evolving existing ideas into new opportunities. We need big thinkers in our classrooms!

A recent tweet from a creative colleague showed an image of some cardboard packing materials that came with a shipment of mugs. That seems ordinary enough, right? But the uniqueness of the image caught the attention of other makers. He posted the picture and asked the maker community, "What would you make with this?"

Educators and makers posted their creative visions for the uniquely shaped material. Innovative suggestions were shared with many focused on student strengths and interests. The image represented hundreds of possibilities for hacking, recycling, and remaking for a mind that is open to those creative possibilities. That single picture prompted hundreds of creative thoughts from makers, artists, and educators. It represented the fact that we can unlock creativity if we just take time to notice the possibilities around us. There are creative possibilities in our homes, in our neighborhoods, and even in our packing materials!

Creative thinkers observe the world around them and ask curious questions, wondering about the way things work and why. They wonder what is possible or what might be. Creative makers are "what if"-ers.

What if we did this? What if we tried that?

When we engage students in this type of playful learning, they begin to wonder how to accomplish a task and what materials to use. When they are creating, their minds wander into the next idea, the next project, or the next possibility.

When you develop a creative mindset in the classroom, it starts with you, the teacher. Do you have wonderings? Do you share those questions with your students? Do you explore things that you are curious about and tinker with materials? Makers mess with things, and they aren't afraid to get dirty. Is your classroom a place where getting messy is ok?

A creative mindset for students means that all learners are open to creativity in the classroom, and they look to demonstrate that creativity in many different ways. A creative mindset for teachers means that we are open to the possibilities for creative learning and are willing to take that risk in the classroom. As we develop a creative mindset within our students and ourselves, it is important to look for possibilities to incorporate creative moments into our instruction.

FUEL CREATIVE THINKERS

"Come in, Dr. Maslyk! You're gonna want to see what we're working on," Aubrey, a third-grade student said to me as I stood in the doorway to her classroom. She was working at a café style table, standing with two classmates. There were some sketches out on the table, and the group was hovering around talking intently about their task. They were building some sort of structure with Lincoln Logs. "We're designing a new reading nook," another student told me. "This is our prototype, and we're gonna see if we can actually build it!"

What started out as play turned into a hands-on project driven by a small group of students. Their enthusiasm was evident, but that is what happens when you give 8-year-olds ownership over their learning. No prompting. No teacher facilitation. Just the opportunity to create something. The students in this example aren't preparing for the state test, they're building skills for life. They are designing and problem-solving in ways that not only connect to curriculum but are driven by play.

Creative thinkers engage in processes in the classroom. They ponder over the writing process or dive into the engineering and design process. Creative thinkers consider the steps it takes to create pottery or make paper or solve a complex math problem. Each creative process can look unique for different individuals, with some learners designing their own personalized pathway to creativity, much like the third-grade innovators mentioned above. This creative cycle happens when learners are at play, but we can also set up these same conditions within the classroom to promote creative thinking and hands-on learning when we bring awareness to the creative cycle.

INSPIRATION-EXPLORATION-MAKE-REFLECT-SHARE

If you have a creative mindset, you know how it feels when you feel that first tingle of inspiration. It's that *a-ha* moment when an idea strikes you and gets your creative juices flowing. The inspiration fuels individuals with a creative mindset for making, and it compels them to move through the creative cycle. They imagine and begin to doodle, sketch a draft of their idea, and soon explore the materials needed to create it. The processing of making can take time and often means that the creator returns back to other parts of the cycle, revisiting their inspiration or looking back at their original plan. Reflection may happen throughout the creative cycle as learners ponder their choices. Reflection also occurs when the project has neared an ending point (because creative makers are never really finished with their idea). Our young makers think about what they've created (a poem, a cake, a tower, a drawing) and they wonder how they can make it better. Sometimes things need to be tweaked, added, or subtracted. Creative thinkers want to improve their craft, so they share their work with others to get feedback, to see their reaction, to enjoy the creation together.

The process of creating isn't just about the final product, though. It starts from the first spark of inspiration when learners are struck with a creative idea. They play with the idea, unravel and reconstruct it. It may stay with them for a while. They are often compelled to act on it. Creative makers get going with a design. It might start out as a drawing or a note. It might turn into their masterpiece. This is the chance to get out the idea that has, up until now, only been in their imagination.

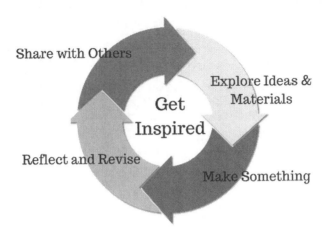

STRATEGIES FOR CREATIVE PLAY

Release untapped creativity in the classroom by fueling curiosity and making time for play. Making in school can happen just about anywhere—in the classroom, in the library, or in the makerspace. How do you ensure that creative play is manageable in the classroom setting? Through maker learning and creative play, there are several strategies that can be used to incorporate this practice in small ways.

A creative mindset highlights three things that innovative thinkers do. When learners become creators, they:

1. Look for possibilities.
2. Love the process.
3. Live for creativity.

On a recent visit to Toronto, I spoke as the keynote for an inaugural STEAM conference which included various workshops as well as an innovation playground in the school library. I expected to find some cool educational toys to tinker with, but I never imagined what I found when I entered the library space, renamed "The Atelier" (meaning workshop or studio). The room was set up by a group of educators and was the most stunning display of light, color, and art!

These educators created an experience for visitors that encompassed all three things that makers do.

The Atelier was carefully designed in a way that enticed you to look for possibilities. The room was dimly lit, drawing you in closer, inviting you to engage with the hands-on materials. Moving through the space, there were student-created shadow boxes using Little Bits to create light and movement. There were signs inviting participants to engage with the displays joining in the creative process. Look here. Touch this. Give this a try. It was the epitome of a creative playground.

How do we do this in our classrooms? I don't mean to transform your room into an Atelier, although that would certainly spark creativity. Consider how you are designing educational experiences that entice students into hands-on, creative learning in a playful way.

On one table of the Atelier, a note asked: "How do color and movement inspire you?" Strategically positioned around the display were books by Hervé Tullet, *The Game of Light* and *The Game of Dark* next to a lit display that welcomed visitors to touch and manipulate the light in a lightbox.

Colored stones and sand sat atop a mirror with a dimly lit string of lights around it. Boldly colored acrylic pinwheels and transparent tangram pieces were scattered about. A rainbow lightbox had been built from scratch through a partnership with the industrial arts teacher. Tables were filled with opportunities to dive into the creative process and make something, as every display pulled you in. The Atelier was an invitation for visitors to touch, tinker, and explore; a true example of what it meant to live in creativity.

The creative mindset can be fostered in the way we design our learning spaces and plan our instruction. How do we encourage our students to look for the creative possibilities in the things around them? In what ways do we engage our students in creative processes that will build their creative agility? Do we give all learners the opportunity to engage deeply in tasks so that they develop a love of innovation and a hunger for creativity? Let's take a look at creative possibilities and the ways we can unlock this strategy in our classrooms.

LOOK FOR POSSIBILITIES

The first step in looking for possibilities is opening our minds to what is around us. Think about how our surroundings represent possibilities for creative play. Consider the maker materials we have access to in our schools and how these might present possibilities for exploration. Opportunities to create, try new materials, or invent new things are examples of how we look for possibilities and make time for play. If you aren't sure what this creative strategy might look like in action, let's look at one example that sparks creative agility and at times can also provide some comic relief in the classroom.

Maker Improv is a quick idea can be used with both kids and adults. We think about improvisation in the theater as the actors are quickly thrown into an experience without any preparation. It pushes the individuals to think on their feet and often devise creative responses to their fellow actors. Improvisation can also be a playful way to engage learners of all ages in creative brainstorming in the classroom.

Here's how Maker Improv works:

In a medium-sized gift bag, prepare a variety of small, random items (to provide about a dozen items per bag). You might include household items like a measuring cup, a coffee filter, a clothespin, or some aluminum foil. Incorporate classroom supplies like a wooden block, dice, or a bookmark. Arts and crafts items are also great to include, like beads, feathers, clay, or fabric scraps. You can also include items from the outdoors like small rocks, a pinecone, seeds, or even a leaf.

Standing in a circle, gather small groups of 8-10 people. One at a time, each individual pulls one item out of the mystery bag and quickly has to determine what they imagine it to be. You may provide a sentence starter like, "It's not a _____, it's a _____." For example, I might pull out a paper clip and say, "it's not a paper clip, it's a key," and model how the key might open an imaginary door. It requires quick thinking with unknown, but familiar objects. Sometimes improv tasks may feel uncomfortable. (Often it is adult learners who feel uneasy with improv tasks. Students don't often demonstrate this same hesitation.) It pushes us into some creative struggle as we are on the spot trying to come up with a creative response. This type of task helps to build our creative muscles, thinking outside the box and thinking about creative possibilities.

Make sure each participant gets a turn. You will start to see the nervousness fade away as it's replaced with smiles and laughter. Hesitant improv participants will shift into innovative thinkers and silly storytellers. When you think the group is ready, then add a challenging twist to the activity:

- Send the bag around a second time with each person choosing another item. Then everyone has to come up with a new idea that combines the two items together.
- Have people pair up and combine their items, co-creating a new design, and use for the items.
- Instead of pulling an additional item, have everyone pass their item to the person on the right. Now come up with a different possibility for the item that was passed to you.

This activity could serve as a getting to know you activity with students nudging thinking and pushing the boundaries of their comfort zone. It is a playful and quick way for learners to start thinking creatively about ordinary things around them and finding new and interesting uses for items. This could also be a strategy for educator professional development. Improv can spark the imagination of teachers and get their ideas flowing. Active learning opportunities like this can be an effective way to foster collaboration and conversation with learners of all ages!

Following an improv activity, engage learners in creative writing, design challenges, or other creativity-centered activities to continue to develop the thinking that occurs during improv. How do you envision using Maker Improv in the classroom? Brainstorm a list of items you can use for this creativity-building activity.

MAKER IMPROV

_____

_____

_____

_____

_____

_____

_____

_____

ASK CURIOUS QUESTIONS

Another way to look for possibilities in the world around us is by asking curious questions. If you have your own children at home (or perhaps teach 25 of them in the classroom), you know the very common sound of, "Ugh, I'm bored! I don't know what to do!" Sadly, kids say this all the time. How that is possible with all of the things that learners can do and explore is beyond me. However, we can engage our students in playful thinking activities to expand their thinking and promote the development of creative ideas.

My sons are ages five and seven. They are pretty active kids and enjoy doing lots of different things, but they too will shout out their occasional boredom. Sometimes, I choose to let that feeling linger a bit. Letting them be bored allows their minds to wander. I try to take advantage of those opportunities and ask them some curious questions. Sometimes we just lay on the floor looking up at the ceiling and laugh as we come up with our outrageously curious questions and even sillier answers.

What would happen if:

- all the trees were blue?
- there were no more pets?
- cars could only drive in reverse?
- books were the new currency?
- all roads were made of sand?

What would it be like if two unlike things were combined like:

- turtles and giraffes?
- spaghetti and ice cream?
- birds and chairs?
- cars and beds?

These curious questions can be purely imaginative or may link to an opportunity to make and invent. What could we invent if we combined two unrelated objects:

- markers and scissors?
- a backpack and an umbrella?
- a purse and a phone charger?

Just think about some of the technologies that have been invented in the last 10 years that may have come from asking curious questions and playing with unusual ideas. What would happen if we combined a computer and a watch? Shoes and roller-skates? How might we combine a spoon and a fork or a hat with a cup holder? These unusual mashups resulted in new inventions. Imagine the curious combinations your students could come up with if allowed to play with ideas.

Asking curious questions is an activity that you can do at home with your own children or at school with your students as a way to unlock creative potential. This can be a morning warm-up activity, a creative writing prompt, or a homework assignment that can generate curious thinking at home. It can be an individual task or a small group discussion. Creative writing and artwork can also extend from this simple questioning activity. In the midst of boredom are sparks of creativity, just waiting to be ignited when we ask students curious questions. Creative conversations that come out of playful questions can be a springboard to student designs, inventions, and collaborative thinking that can foster creative agility in the classroom.

LOVE THE PROCESS

Playful learners love the process of exploring, tinkering, creating, and all that goes with it. The stumbling blocks. The exhilarating a-ha moments. The quiet time for brainstorming. The noisy time for making, hammering, constructing, and hacking.

When students engage in hands-on learning, they begin to appreciate the creative process. They recognize that making takes time and energy. Though students might get discouraged when they encounter a setback, they possess the perseverance to push through it. Student makers might jot their ideas down in a sketchbook or write it on a sticky note. They let it incubate for a while and revisit it with imaginative elaboration.

The creative process will look different for everyone. Think about what your personal creative process looks like. Share it with your students, so they can develop a process that will work for them. Here's a way that you can discover some creative processes together:

- Research the creative processes of others. Read about how Jackson Pollock created his paintings or how Dr. Seuss found his unique story ideas.
- Watch a creative process in action. Watch a sketchnote artist as she doodles and connects ideas or pull up a video of a marching band as they're practicing.
- Interview others about their creative process. Think about those within your school or in the community who could share their creative process with you and your students.

The process of creating and making is often isolated to the art room, but with the inclusion of makerspaces in many schools we are now expanding the opportunities for students to express themselves through the process of designing, making, and iterating. Whether you engage in creativity in a dedicated space, the hallway, or outside on the sidewalk, students can engage in the creative process just about anywhere.

EMBED OPPORTUNITIES TO PLAY

Creating opportunities to play in our schools is another key to unlocking creativity. When we develop a creative mindset in our students, we unlock possibilities for them to create. As students become makers, builders, and designers, their creative mindset is nurtured. Through informal play and tinkering, learners thrive on opportunities to create in any form. Cooking, sculpture, dance, or design, makers with a creative mindset look for opportunities to uncover bold ideas and try something new. These ideas may be unfamiliar or unconventional at times but provide the chance for learners to engage in the creative cycle and nurture their creative mindset.

CREATIVE CONSIDERATIONS

Play is an opportunity to create. It is the chance to think and explore in ways that may lead to increased curiosity and creative invention. Making time to play will look different in every classroom. We can be playful in the questions we ask and in the projects we assign. Reflect on one way you will encourage students to look for possibilities this week, within your classroom, around the school, or in their neighborhood. When we recognize what is possible, our creative minds begin to imagine the pathway to bring that idea to fruition. What strategies will you unleash to make time for play?

INVITATIONS TO IMAGINATION

Making time for play in the classroom is an important step toward unlocking student creativity.   Play allows us to explore possibilities and engage in creative processes that nurture innovative thinking within our students.

• Think of one way you might incorporate the idea an atelier-style area of the classroom that can be used for exploration and making.

• Practice a creative round of improv in your classroom this week.

• Brainstorm a list of curious questions and embed them into some upcoming lessons.

• Post a picture of an unusual image or material on social media using #UnlockCreativity. Ask your learning network, what can your students create with this?

BE A CREATIVE CHAMPION

 Every child deserves a champion: an adult who will never give up on them, who understands the power of connection and insists that they become the best they can possibly be. — Rita Pearson

SHARE YOUR PASSION

Fred Rogers was a champion for children. He was passionate about creating a children's television program that was deliberate, honest, and different. Every episode, every interaction that Mr. Rogers had with his audience and with his real-life neighbors was one that focused on the hearts and minds of children. His deep belief in spreading kindness and creating playful encounters for young people permeated through our television screens and into our homes.

Fred Rogers was an innovator, pushing the limits of what was expected and creating something meaningful and long-lasting. He was a good neighbor, reaching out to his community and reaching into the households of families each day. He did whatever it took to share his message and connect with others.

Just as Fred Rogers served as an advocate for children from our TV screens all the way to Congress, we too need to be champions for our students. We can be advocates for learning opportunities that will prompt creativity. We can be intentional about designing the types of learning that will not only meet the needs of our students, but also engage them in creative thinking, collaboration, and design. Within our classrooms, we have a responsibility to create the conditions that will spark new ideas within our students and tap into their interests. This might happen through coding, STEAM learning, or creative challenges. It can happen as we change our learning environments to meet the needs of our students or when we let them make creative decisions in the classroom. We must be the champions of this work.

As we demonstrate our belief in creative thinking in our classrooms, we elevate its importance. We can promote creativity by making it a priority within the curriculum and through our instructional decisions. When we convey that we are passionate about supporting our students as creators and innovators, this message should resonate through all that we do. As champions for creativity, we can develop connected learning experiences that require exploration, problem-solving, and creative thinking. This will look different in every classroom, but there are ways we can share our passion for creativity while developing engaging learning experiences for our students.

Consider the following creative project. Students have designed a miniature model of an eco-friendly building. They've researched solar panels and considered ways to make their model "green." They've calculated and measured each piece of the building to meet the specified dimensions. Teams discussed the materials they needed to build a strong structure. One building even has an elevator, which the students have developed using a DC mini motor. They've incorporated circuits to create lighting and used programming skills to install a motion sensor alarm at the front door. The tabletop designs include landscaping around the outside and a welcoming entrance. Students have considered all the details in the planning of this building project.

This middle school project has been a semester-long experience, culminating in a public presentation of each building design. The students have collaborated, constructed, deconstructed, designed, and redesigned. They have tapped into their knowledge from math classes, science labs, and art courses to accomplish their task, using communication skills to work as a team and critical thinking to make decisions. They have unlocked their creativity and are ready to share their passion with a panel of experts who provide feedback and support to this integrated learning experience.

Educators who are creative champions call attention to creative thinking like this. They expose students to learning opportunities that will require a creative mindset, and that will test creative stamina. A creative champion coaches learners in their creativity and cheers them on as they build on their successes.

PUSH PROBLEM-SOLVING

If we want students to think creatively, then we need to present them with interesting problems that need solving. Complex problems exist everywhere, and many don't have clear solutions. Part of our responsibility is to prepare students to identify and apply innovative solutions to the problems in our society, but some students struggle with the ability to grapple with such challenges. As creative champions, we can expose students to the kind of problem-solving that will equip them with the unique skills and dispositions needed as we prepare them for the work of the future.

Inquiry and discovery in science, innovation in technology or creativity through the arts -opportunities like these allow students to think abstractly and uncover possible solutions to real-world problems. As the lead learner in our classrooms, we can provide opportunities for collaboration as learners tackle new challenges that require creative thinking. When students share ideas or build something together, new insights are generated in a way that will prepare students for what happens beyond their K-12 school experience.

Adopting a problem-solving approach may require a different role for teachers, from leader to facilitator, from director to coach, and from observer to champion. We can support problem-solving in the way we ask students questions, push them to look for patterns, explain their thoughts, and defend their decisions. We are championing their creativity when we place our students in challenging learning experiences that will encourage them to think differently about problems and use their skills to come up with viable solutions.

When educators step back so that students can lead the problem-solving task, there are many benefits to students. Through this process, they:

- Learn from other perspectives.
- Collaborate with others.
- Overcome challenges.
- Build self-confidence.
- Increase creative thinking processes.

The global economy is changing, and students need to prepare for college, career, and beyond. The skills students are building with a focus on a creative mindset will help them to solve the unknown problems of the future. As champions of their future, we can take steps to prepare students by building critical skills like problem-solving, collaboration, and creativity.

SET UP STUDENTS FOR SUCCESS

If we are going to lift up creative learning in our schools, then we need to step up and be creative champions ready to embed these future-ready skills into our teaching. Each day, we have the opportunity in every classroom to build up our students as creative thinkers. Sometimes it takes time to help students recognize that they have creative talents, but it is our job as champions to identify these strengths and bring attention to them. We can support learners as they build creative habits and notice creative possibilities around them. We can design lessons that will set students up for critical thinking and creative problem-solving. We can design our learning environments in ways that promote creative success for every student that crosses our path.

As creative champions for our learners, we are their cheerleaders, advocating for the learning that will best serve them in the future. We can amplify our students' creative voices when we are designing instruction and developing curriculum so that student creativity is a common thread throughout our courses. Common assessments that include options for creative thinkers and tools that can support creativity in the classroom need to be shared in educational conversations.

Championing the success of our students can happen through the intentional choices we make within the curriculum, but also through the personal ways we acknowledge and support creative learners. When we value creative expression and out of the box thinking, we recognize these as assets within our students. We give students feedback on their growth and development as creative individuals. We show them through our words and actions what a letter grade doesn't begin to express.

Don't miss the opportunity to carve out a creative path for your students. Look for ways that you can highlight student creativity in your school. When we accept the role of a creative champion, we are committing to growing our students as creative, productive citizens whose ideas will result in new inventions, global solutions, and works of art.

BE INTENTIONAL ABOUT DESIGNING THE TYPES OF LEARNING THAT WILL NOT ONLY MEET THE NEEDS OF YOUR STUDENTS, BUT ALSO ENGAGE THEM IN CREATIVE THINKING AND COLLABORATION.

PATHWAYS FOR CREATIVE LEARNING

Fred Rogers was so passionate about his show *Mr. Roger's Neighborhood* that he felt compelled to share it with anyone who would listen. A humble promoter, he looked for ways to share why the content was important and how it was building positive relationships in and around communities. His work represented a pathway for creative thinking and personal connections that allowed him to shine a light on the education and development of young children.

We need to step up and be creative champions so we can promote the passionate work of our students. If a pathway doesn't currently exist, this is your opportunity to blaze a trail—design ways within your classroom for students to explore creative learning and develop skills that will allow them to be successful in the future. Providing guidance and encouragement as champions will help our students to seize the opportunity to unlock their creativity.

CREATIVITY POWER CARDS

Being a champion for creativity may mean providing guidance and support to students who need it. Within your classroom, you may have reluctant students who are creative thinkers in the making. They might need some support as they take on this new role as designer, creator, programmer, and maker. Getting them to dig into the process of creative thinking may take some support at first. Sometimes a bit of structure can help guide students through the process.

Kids love trading cards. Baseball cards. Pokémon cards. They organize the cards, study them, trade them with their friends. Let's capitalize on that interest and design a way for students to find some creative inspiration.

Suppose you are getting ready for a small group activity. Maybe you are presenting a design challenge to the class for the first time and feel more comfortable with some guidelines. Students can learn about some of the "hats" that creators wear when they are in the midst of an innovative project.

The Imaginative Thinker

Imaginative Thinkers are the dreamers and the idea generators. These are our students who need to be brought back to the task, as they are often in a daydream. Although we may think they aren't paying attention, they may just be lost in their own world of creative thinking. Give them the time and support to develop their ideas and the tools to make them a reality.

This might be a card with an image of a brain, the statue of Rodin's Thinker, or a character that students might associate with imaginative thinking like Wile E. Coyote. Be sure to check out Creative Commons for free images and be aware of copyright violations when using trademarked characters and images.

The Artistic Designer

Artistic designers are creative doodlers and planners who can take the idea from the imaginative thinkers and propel it into action. These students have their notebooks filled with ideas, the cover included. They often sketch, sometimes to maintain their focus. Never overlook the Artistic Designer's ability to make learning visible and give them strategies to demonstrate it in the classroom. The power card for the creative designer might feature a Picasso-like painting or a picture of Bob Ross painting some "happy little trees."

The Digital Dynamo

Our tech-savvy students need the chance to show their creativity in a digital form. The Digital Dynamo might add creativity through virtual

DIGITAL DYNAMO

These tech-savvy learners can transfer their creativity into any digital form. They connect tech to creative thinking in innovative ways.

#UNLOCKCREATIVITY

reality or video animation. This is our student who always has his head down in a device. He is the first volunteer to try a new tech tool or troubleshoot when tech goes wrong in class. Give Digital Dynamos the opportunity to use their expertise positively, connecting tech to creativity and ensuring their voice is heard. This power card might show a picture of a computer, an AI robot, or other popular digital character.

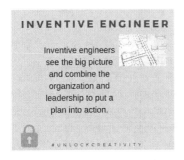

INVENTIVE ENGINEER

Inventive engineers see the big picture and combine the organization and leadership to put a plan into action.

#UNLOCKCREATIVITY

The Inventive Engineer

The Inventive Engineers combine the work of the thinkers, designer, and techies as they execute the plan. This student often emerges as a group leader wanting to create a blueprint or map out the plan. Though the plan may be a little unconventional, the Inventive Engineer has an innovative back-up plan ready to go! Use creative challenges as a chance for these students to step up as project managers and lead others in a productive way. These creative inventors can be represented by Inspector Gadget or Iggy Peck Architect. Students can even design the cards themselves and choose an image that represents the ideals behind being an inventive engineer.

CREATIVE STORYTELLER

Whether through writing or telling, creative storytellers find imaginative ways to share their ideas with others.

#UNLOCKCREATIVITY

The Creative Storyteller

Every creative project has a story to tell. The Creative Storyteller has strong communication skills, and is always ready to write, tell a story, or figure out a way to share their ideas with others. Support creativity by guiding them to use this strength, and the storyteller will excel in this role. The storyteller card is a reminder that the details in your creativity can be shared with others. This creativity card might have a speech bubble on it or a picture of a story-teller that your students identify with. It might even include an image of one of the students!

The image can be whatever or whoever may be relevant to your students based on their grade, subject, or general background. Better yet, have your students design the cards for the classroom! The idea is that the card can serve as a quick reminder when they are preparing for a creative task or getting ready to work with a collaborative group on a project.

Some students may possess many of these traits, while they may be hard to see in others. As a creative champion, tease out these qualities in your students so they can be creators and contributors, not merely consumers. Creativity Power Cards can be made out of cardstock and used in different ways. Here's how you might use power cards in your classroom:

- Use the cards as a prompt to remind students of the characteristics we need to activate when we are focusing on our creative mindset.
- The cards can also be selected by students or assigned to students when working on a collaborative or creative task. Students who don't consider themselves as creative can use their card as their way to contribute. Sometimes students need to focus in on one aspect of creative design. The cards can be a way to show students that everyone can provide an aspect of creativity to their work.
- The cards could also be used as a way to recognize the creative efforts of students. When the "Imaginative Thinker" really helped to propel an idea forward, you could award that student a card to highlight the way they demonstrated their creative agility in the classroom.

Creativity Power Cards are just one way that you can encourage students to tap into all aspects of their creative genius. Have an idea for a different creative power? Add it to the list! Don't think that the cards will work for you or your students? That's OK. There are lots of other ways to engage learners in the creative process and develop creative thinking skills like inventors, designers, and makers.

PUT IT OUT THERE

When we accept the role of creative champion, we have a responsibility to share the importance of creativity with those around us. We can reach out to those who are in our schools and our local communities, as well as sharing with those in our global network. Use the power of your connected network to promote the creative work of your students. Put out the word about creativity in both low—and high-tech ways, calling attention to the creative minds within our classrooms.

As creative champions, we need to tell the story of student success. We may already do this to some extent, sharing classroom creativity with our colleagues or posting student work in the hallways of our schools, but we can do much more. Let's use our own creativity to spread the word and get others noticing the importance of creativity through the way we promote the work of our students.

Here are some ways to put it into action:

- Use student artwork or photos of their creations as the landing page image for your class website. Consider a caption that calls attention to creativity, and make it a monthly feature.
- Choose a piece of student work as your screensaver. Imagine how proud students will feel when they see their work on your phone or classroom device.
- Select creative pieces of student work to share with parents and community. Images of student work can be made into greeting cards or calendars that can be used as a fundraiser to bring more creative materials into your school or simply as a way to champion classroom creativity.
- Can't capture creativity in a single image? Try a video. Create a

two-minute video of a classroom gallery walk showing off student projects or a classroom performance. Post the video to your class or district website to share with others.

- Share the creative habits that you and your class have developed over the last several weeks. Send an idea out in a tweet or through a class blog.
- Use tools like Smore or Google Slides to create a digital newsletter as another way to make others aware of the creative stamina being built in your classroom.

When we put it out there, we are letting those in our network know that our students have something important to share. We have an opportunity to amplify the creative voices of our students by using our resources and abilities to serve as advocates for this work. As we highlight student creativity, we are stepping up as champions of their work and calling on others to do the same. How will you put it out there for others? Take some notes or sketch some ideas that will be used to tell your creative story.

YOUR CREATIVE STORY

_____
_____
_____
_____
_____
_____
_____
_____
_____
_____

MAKE IT PERSONAL

Being a champion for creativity means that we are responsible for promoting the creative work of those around us in big and small ways. This might mean publicly celebrating the work of our students or sharing the innovative practices of our colleagues. Celebrating the creative strides of your students doesn't always have to be a public display or large event. We can celebrate creativity in small, subtle ways as well. Your acknowledgment might be just what that student needed to keep pursuing an idea or trying a new creative strategy. This can be as simple as a sticky note of encouragement. Taking the time to hand-write a message to a student can go a long way toward their creative confidence. As advocates, we can create personalized opportunities that can lift up student creativity in ways that nurture student development and champion individual successes.

- Keep a package of blank cards or notes in your desk. Write a positive message to three students every day. These can be just two or three sentences. Over a few weeks, you can reach out to every student in your class, letting them know that you see creativity in them.
- Share a message of encouragement on the board for the class. This can be a quote about creativity or a positive message about the collective creativity of the class.
- Send some creative praise home. Every parent will appreciate a positive note about their child, especially if you take the time to personally write it, as opposed to emailing. Just a few lines to say, "Johnny has been thinking creatively in class. You should see his most recent project! Just thought you should know that he is doing a great job." Parents will love that you've noticed something special about their child and took the time to share it in a personalized way.

Making the celebration personal provides students with positive feedback from you. They will know that their creative efforts are valued and appreciated, which is important since we don't always acknowledge this type of growth. Knowing that they have a creative champion in you is critical to their ongoing development as a creative learner.

CREATIVITY NOTEBOOK

In my former role as an elementary principal, I was fortunate to work in a small community with supportive and engaged families. Parents and community members were always in the building to volunteer in the classrooms, attend school events, or just stop by to say hello.

I had a positive relationship with many parents and communicated with them often. One afternoon while conducting a teacher observation, I just had to take a moment to reach out to a parent.

The class was designing marble roller coaster tracks and one team's design was just extraordinary. I grabbed my phone and recorded a video of their innovative project in action and sent it to one mom.

"Just wanted you to know that Simon's group is doing some amazingly creative work today and I wanted to share!"

When she stopped into the office after school that day, she was tearing up. The power of a personal message lifted her up as a parent and provided a sense of pride for the student.

FIND THE CHAMPION IN YOU

Everyone needs a champion, that special someone who is rooting for them. You are the creative champion for your students. Carve a path for creative options within your classroom but also look beyond it for ways that you can support the success of your students. Whether through a personalized note or a school-wide shout-out, we are the cheerleaders that our students need.

As we encourage, nudge, and celebrate the creative attempts of our students, we have a responsibility to share this with others. Our voices show others in our school and educational communities that creativity is important to the academic, social, and emotional development of our learners. Be the voice championing creativity. Be the one supporting the creative endeavors of your students. They are counting on you!

CREATIVE CONSIDERATIONS

Being a creative champion for students can happen within your classroom through the ways you structure creative opportunities. It can be through the sharing and promotion of student accomplishments. Not every student will want a loud cheering section, so be sure to choose public and personal ways to let your students know that their creative journey is worth it! Reflect on the ways that you will step up, champion creativity, and advocate for your budding designers, architects, and innovative thinkers. What is one small step you can take to champion the creativity of your students? What pathways already exist for promoting and uplifting the work of creative learners? Or will you create your own path?

INVITATIONS TO IMAGINATION

We can serve as creative champions in ways that provide opportunities within the classroom and in the ways that we raise up the work of our students beyond the classroom. The positive steps that we take can have an impact on our students and their creative journey.

• Try a structured way to facilitate creative thinking in the classroom by developing your own Creativity Power Cards.

• Promoting the creative accomplishments of your class is the job of a creative champion. Work with your students to select one way that you will share creativity with others through videos, newsletters, or social media.

• Write down personal, positive messages for three of your students and their families as a way to show that you are always in their corner.

THINK DIFFERENTLY

 Creativity requires the courage to let go of certainty.

— Erich Fromm

OPPORTUNITIES TO GRAPPLE

A couple of years ago, a particular dress hit the media, not because it was from a specific designer or because a famous celebrity wore it to a red-carpet event. The dress garnered millions of views and caused arguments at dinner tables across the world because some people saw it in blue and black tones while others adamantly saw gold and white. We grappled with what felt like a brain teaser as we tried to see it "the other way." The struggle was real. Try as we might, we just couldn't think differently about that dress.

There are similar dilemmas within education, as we may struggle to think differently about our educational system or our instructional practices. Pushing ourselves to think differently about our roles and responsibilities may be challenging at times (almost as challenging as seeing that dress). Adjusting our instructional choices to meet the needs of creative and diverse students may also cause us to think differently about what learning can look like in our classrooms.

We can think differently about our classroom spaces and about our assessment procedures. We can think differently about our technology use and make improvements based on the changing needs of our students. As we ponder these challenges, we may grapple with decisions and struggle to see different perspectives, but we must remember that our students are also faced with similar challenges.

 Thinking differently means that we may need to let go of things we know and are familiar with, and take a risk as we try something new. Thinking differently may mean putting ourselves in someone else's shoes and learning from their perspective. We can design experiences for our students that build empathy and understanding, which allows them to think differently about their learning, themselves, and each other.

Consider this classroom example as a way for students to expand their thinking and grapple with decision-making. When given a chance to participate in a design challenge, one group of students was able to think differently about their role as creative designers.

"I'm thinking that I'll add a hidden pocket on the inside because I know Adam likes to keep his house key in his wallet."

"Jenna is always using her Chapstick, so I need to make sure that I include some kind of feature that will hold it for her."

"I'm not sure what kind of material to use for Maddie's wallet because I know that she wants something lightweight for when she goes jogging."

The students were working on wallet designs for a classmate. Each had to interview their "client" and gather information about their likes and dislikes. They listened carefully for specific needs or desired features. They asked lots of questions of one another, taking notes as they went along. The student designers considered the needs of their classmates and sketched at least two different designs for them. They conferred with their clients again to get feedback on their proposed wallet designs. They also shared their ideas with others on the design team to gather suggestions.

Students then used materials from the makerspace including fabric, Velcro, cardboard, and duct tape to take their designs from sketches to reality. They created a prototype of their design and sought out additional feedback. Some made revisions, making their best attempts to create a design that was functional but also met the needs of the person they were designed for. The project culminated a few days later when the class did a gallery walk viewing all of the wallet designs.

The students didn't get any actual instruction on wallet construction, although they did explore some designs online and looked critically at their own wallets. They weren't certain how things should function or what tools to use to put things together. They were simply presented a challenge and got to work.

The class had done some work on design thinking practices and creative problem-solving. They worked through the design process of brainstorming, questioning, prototyping, and testing. Their teachers embedded four strategies into their classroom practices to help build student thinking and design skills:

- Think across boundaries.
- Create prototypes.
- Seek authentic feedback.
- Share your story.

Students engaged in thinking exercises that stretched across subject areas and beyond the field of education, tapping into history, knowledge of business, and community. They worked on building models, systems, and prototypes within the classroom utilizing a feedback loop. They participated in small and large group discussions building interpersonal and presentation skills so that they could effectively share their stories with others.

The most powerful foundation for this work was realizing that designing for others starts with empathy. It's grappling with different ideas, making decisions for someone else, working to understand the needs of others, and then designing solutions to meet them. This can be a challenge for students because it often means taking a chance that something within the design will fail.

CREATIVE RISK-TAKING

Invent, repurpose, build, hack, design. These are the new descriptors for teaching and learning in schools. No longer are compliance and test scores going to dictate our narratives. We simply can't afford for that to happen. If you believe that the creative citizens of the world are the ones who will solve the problems of our future, then we must fuel their creativity and all that it requires.

With bold creativity comes possible failure. Expressing our creativity represents a multitude of risks. Will my creativity be accepted by others? Will my creative solution solve the problem? Can I be brave enough the share my idea? There is an inherent risk that comes with saying, "I have a design that will improve _____," because we're conveying could be perceived as the original product, task, or experience wasn't "good enough" before. That's why thinking and design are critical to the creative development of our students.

When we think creatively and engage in design, we are putting ourselves out there! That's a risk. Taking that leap into the unknown is scary, but we must model this for our students. If we are creative risk-takers, our students will feel more comfortable with failure and taking risks too. Talk to your students about why different types of learning feel risky. Whether stepping up in a leadership role or taking a creative risk in the classroom, students may need to talk about how risk-taking looks and feels. Write down a few questions that will help you to guide a class discussion on what it means for learners to take risks.

TAKING RISKS

Creative risk means trying an unconventional solution to a problem or sharing out-of-the-box thinking with their peers. Using unusual materials or sharing a creative habit might seem quirky to others, but when we create a classroom environment that supports creative risk-taking, students will embrace failure and begin to develop a creative mindset.

DEVELOP A CREATIVE MINDSET

In conventional classrooms, teachers possess the knowledge and share it with students. In creative classrooms, everyone has the creative knowledge to share. When we engage students in thinking and design practices, we are helping to develop their creative mindset. Not only does thinking about design further our creative agility, but it also instills in students the confidence to say, "My ideas are worth it, and they can change the world!"

Creative students can change the world with the ideas that they develop or the products and technologies they create. It is through the creative process that they will build the dispositions associated with the creative mindset. Thinking flexibly and persevering through obstacles, will not only help students now, but throughout their lives.

Experience in design will help students to look creatively at everyday problems and see themselves as problem solvers. Design doesn't always mean that students are inventing something tangible, although that may be an outcome. Students can design systems to solve problems or experiences for others to engage in. Student designs can result in a physical creation, a blueprint, a flowchart, a menu, an advertisement, or more. By engaging students in creative thinking and design, we are opening up the possibility to rethink and redesign just about anything!

WITH BOLD CREATIVITY COMES POSSIBLE FAILURE.

CREATIVITY NOTEBOOK

Have you ever sat and observed a group of preschoolers or kindergarten students as they work and play? You'll see the carefree way that they interact, talk, and laugh.

There are no preconceived ideas about what their work should look like or what they should be trying to accomplish.

When I watch my sons, I see this same carefree attitude. They aren't afraid to try new things or look at things in a different way. They take unconventional materials and use them in unique ways. They aren't afraid to fail or mess something up. I love that about this age!

I worry though that we "school" that out of them. As we work to foster creativity in our classrooms, let's never lose sight of the carefree ways that our youngest learners embrace failure and find joy in new learning.

SPARK STUDENT THINKING

Who is doing most of the thinking in your classroom, you or your students? We know they can lead learning. We know they can collaborate. With your help, they are building their creative agility every day. We have to let them grapple with the thinking that supports this creative learning process and engage them in activities that promote the development of new ideas and exploring unknown problems.

Here are four strategies that teachers can implement to embed creative thinking and design into any subject area:

1. Pair creative options with subject area content.
2. Incorporate hands-on, collaborative tasks.
3. Provide access to creative materials and resources.
4. Allow time and space for sharing and reflection.

Creativity can be magnified further when several of these strategies are combined together. Think about a common maker project like a marble run or a Rube Goldberg device (an overly complex mechanism to complete a simple task). The reasons why many teachers like to use these challenges is because they tie in multiple strategies. Critical content in math and science can be incorporated into Rube Goldberg devices—ramps, pulleys, angles, speed, measurement. So, we are adding a creative layer to the existing course content.

While the hands-on challenge could be done independently, it provides an opportunity for a small group of students to collaborate and tackle it together. To complete the challenge, students will need access to recycled materials like cardboard, cups, plastic containers, and string. These everyday materials can be used in creative ways to accomplish a complex task. Once the devices are designed, built, and reviewed, it's time to test it. Did it work? Does the design need to be adjusted? Reflecting on the design can help students to look critically at their own work.

Developing these learning experiences for students takes time and effort on the part of creative teachers. Tasks can be connected to curriculum or community and can be designed to serve individuals or groups. Planning for creative thinking and design might mean scouring the web or connecting with other creatives on social media. This chapter will provide a few ways to incorporate creative thinking and design into your classroom.

REMEMBER MAD LIBS?

Creating design challenges is one way to embed creative thinking and design into your classroom. Some teachers naturally think up interesting challenges while others check out Pinterest, Instagram, and Twitter for inspiration. If you are looking for a simple way to challenge your students and get them to think differently, check out my Mad-Libs-inspired prompt. It's a simple way to get kids creating and designing with simple materials.

Did you love Mad Libs when you were younger? Remember the silliness of creating wild stories as you filled in those blank spaces? Random nouns, verbs, and adjectives when combined together created some unusual narratives. As kids, we loved making up silly stories and embraced the ability to create whatever we wanted. Creating with Mad Libs was the chance to concoct a wild story while collaborating with our friends. Let's take the idea of Mad Libs and add a design thinking spin on it.

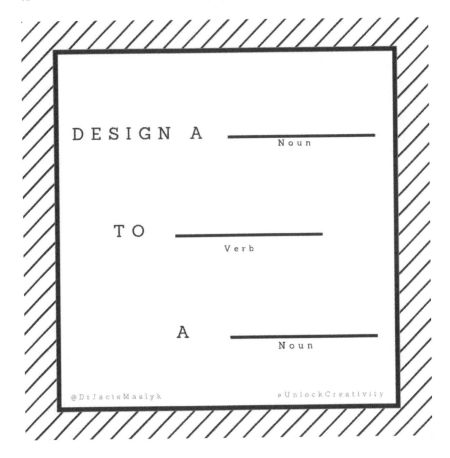

DESIGN A _____
                    Noun

TO _____
        Verb

A _____
        Noun

@DrJacieMaslyk   #UnlockCreativity

Here's how it works:

- Use the Mad Libs prompt and have students name two nouns and one verb. These words will plug into the Mad Libs template to create a design task. For example:
- Design a car to carry a kitten.
- Design a shoe to fit an action figure.
- Design a boat to transport an elephant.
- Design a structure to hold a water bottle.
- Provide students with a variety of simple building materials.
- Newspaper, tape, aluminum foil, tissue paper, pipe cleaners, wiki sticks, yarn, plastic recyclables, or cardboard will work well and are low cost.

- Set a time limit for teams or individuals to plan, build, and revise their designs.
- Once all of the designs are completed, take time to reflect and celebrate.

Want to leverage this strategy and increase the impact? Plan grade-level or building-wide design challenges. These can be a great way to expand the learning beyond your classroom and extend it to other educators and learners.

Thinking about taking this school-wide? Our junior high school serves students in grades 5-8. A committee of teachers from all grade levels and disciplines asserted that hands-on learning and design shouldn't be confined to a few classes or programs, so they decided to create school-wide design challenges that included every student. The committee met throughout the school year and over the summer to set up challenges that would incorporate creativity and collaboration, while also exploring core content. One year, the challenges all had an environmental focus:

- Design and build a bird feeder for the school garden using only recyclable materials.
- Research local vegetation, determine possible pests, and design a deterrent that would protect the school garden from these pests.
- Create a blueprint for an outdoor learning space that multiple classes could use. What would it look like? What materials would be needed?

If you are looking to expand your design work across the country and connect with others engaged in design, try the "Ship a Chip" challenge. In this creative design task, students are given one individual potato chip. They must think differently about materials to design a package that will safely ship the chip to a partner class in another school or district. So, while your class is designing and redesigning, they are connecting with another group of students who are engaged in the same project. We'll ship our chips to you. You ship your chips to us. On arrival day, the classrooms can connect via Skype or Google Hangouts to open their packages simultaneously and see which designs were the most successful. If a whole, uncrunched chip arrives then your packaging was a success. A crumbled chip, and students head back to the drawing board.

Design tasks can be as simple or complex as you or your students want to make them. The idea is that student thinking will be challenged as they design for a variety of people and purposes. Challenges can be fun and whimsical or closely tied to curriculum content, and challenges can include simple materials or more detailed plans. What is important is that students feel supported in their creative efforts to think and design in the classroom.

Embed time to reflect on the design tasks and the way that students are building their creative agility through design. As they build creative stamina in the classroom, their changes in thinking may extend into other areas. It might help students to think about ways that design and creativity might allow them to contribute to the well-being of others.

THINK, MAKE, CONTRIBUTE

Designing for others builds empathy and understanding. Designers gain perspective and think differently about problems others may be facing. Engaging learners in empathy-building tasks gives them the chance to think in different ways about problems, solutions, people, and materials. One way to unlock creativity and develop empathy is through community-based problem-finding and problem-solving projects. Students of all ages can think, make, and contribute to their school and community.

You can begin helping learners to build at a very young age. Use the "think, make, contribute" strategy to infuse creative design and empathetic thinking into your classroom.

Here's how it works:

1. Generate a list of problems with your students:

- There aren't enough things to play with during recess.
- The front of our school doesn't feel welcoming.
- There's always lots of garbage at the park in our neighborhood.

1. Allocate time for student teams to brainstorm and sketch possible solutions to the identified problems.
2. Prompt students to look for facts surrounding the problem. Do they need to interview community members, research a website, or talk to the principal to determine the feasibility of solving the problems?
3. Provide students with access to tools and materials to generate potential prototypes connected to their solutions. These could include physical designs or other proposals to address the identified concerns.
4. Reconvene groups so that students can share ideas, ask questions, and give feedback.
5. Revisit and refine the prototypes.
6. Make time for whole class and individual reflection.
7. Celebrate the solutions by sharing with the community or exhibiting the student designs in some way.

There are also problems that exist that your students may not know about. Use this as an opportunity to research current events and global issues that might prompt your students to act. As a creative and connected educator, be on the lookout for ways that your students can get involved with their community by focusing their creative contributions to those in need locally and globally. Brainstorm some ways that your classroom can contribute to the community through design and making.

WAYS TO CONTRIBUTE

_____

_____

_____

One classroom teacher took a community connection that she made and turned it into a maker project that taught students about responsible recycling and giving back. Have you heard of plarn? Plarn is short for plastic yarn and is made from plastic grocery bags. You probably have a ton of them under your kitchen sink. When cut into strips and knotted together, the plastic bags can be turned into purses, hats, shoes, and baskets. Students can create the plarn that can be used in different ways. Check out Instructables[1], a great site that shares how to make plarn (and just about anything else you can think of!).

First, students measure and cut the plastic bags. Then, they need to learn how to weave the plarn. The plarn designs in one classroom went far beyond fashion accessories. Instead, the students decided to create sleeping mats which were donated to a local church and handed out to homeless people in the community. Through the experience, students engaged in hands-on making but also built empathy and understanding about issues impacting their community. Their creative reasoning allowed them to think beyond themselves and design something that had an impact on others.

These students were able to design a physical project that also supported their local community. Not all creative projects need to result in a tangible product. Students can gain experience in creative thinking and design through other types of experiences, too.

DESIGNING INNOVATIVE SYSTEMS AND EXPERIENCES

Design doesn't always have to mean physically making something. Creative thinking and design can alter a process or experience while allowing students to understand the perspectives of others. Thinking differently about existing things allows students to create in new and different ways. It forces students to stretch their ideas beyond what already exists.

Designing innovative systems and experiences may sound complicated, but it is a task that can be done as a way to get students thinking creatively. These design tasks can spark whole class discussion, serve as a creative writing prompt, or turn into a fully hands-on building and design challenge. Posing unique design questions to students provides them with an opportunity to put themselves into another person's shoes while also engaging in design thinking. Here's what designing systems and experiences might this look like in the classroom:

Step 1: Pose one of these questions (or design your own):

- How can you redesign the classroom to make it a more collaborative space?
- How might we redesign an open house to make it more family-friendly?
- What would an amusement park for pets look like?
- How might you plan a birthday party for someone who is visually impaired?
- What considerations would you need to make when designing a Halloween costume for a friend in a wheelchair?
- How might you design a storybook for someone who speaks a different language than you do?
- How would you redesign the experience of a student orientation to high school?
- How might you improve the cafeteria program to make it more efficient, student-friendly, healthier, etc.?

Step 2: Student design teams are provided time to brainstorm ideas around this new system or experience. They might spend time doing research, sketching, or talking about ideas.

Step 3: Teams draft a plan, which can be a written plan, a drawing, or something done digitally. The plan should include special features including an explanation for why the team designed the system the way that they did.

Step 4: Provide time for feedback, consulting with groups, and have them ask questions of one another. This process deepens thinking and often prompts designers to reconsider, revise, and improve their plans.

Step 5: Share your work!

Not only does designing experiences and systems help students to build their own creative agility, but it also empowers them to consider ways to improve the world around them, not only for themselves, but for others. The opportunity to think about complex problems and design potential solutions provides students with the opportunity to collaborate with others, think critically about their environment, and unlock their own creativity while they are designing for social good.

INFUSE CREATIVITY AND DESIGN

We don't always need fancy materials or expensive equipment to create opportunities for our students to think and learn like designers. With intention, we can structure learning opportunities that require learners to grapple with ideas, reframe their thinking, and push them to consider innovative solutions to complex problems. We can carve out time and space for students to engage in design tasks that are structured, silly, and/or student-centered. When learners design, they tap into innovative thinking and creative processes that may aren't always activated in school. The type of learning described in this chapter not only builds creative stamina in our students, but also fosters empathy and understanding throughout the classroom.

CREATIVE CONSIDERATIONS

Every day in the classroom, we have a chance to foster deep thinking and develop creative problem solvers. We can nudge students to think differently through the lessons we design and how we ask students to solve problems. As students grapple with ideas, we can expand their thinking and tap into their creativity. Our students aren't the only ones who can benefit from alternative approaches to thinking.

As creative educators, we can reexamine our teaching practices and develop creative hacks that will provide more opportunities for our students to think, engage, and create in the classroom. How might you reconsider your approach to creativity? What can students gain from thinking like a designer? What steps will you take this week to develop student empathy through design?

INVITATIONS TO IMAGINATION

Now it is time for you and your students to act and think differently. Choose one of the following three options this week to bring about creative thinking and help develop a powerful mindset in the classroom.

• Try the Mad Libs template and see how your students rise up to the challenge to design and build something unique.

• Explore challenges that your community faces. Create a design opportunity that will allow students to build empathy and give back to their community.

• Plan a lesson that will push your students to engage in systems thinking by encouraging them to redesign an existing system or experience.

• Post a systems thinking design question that you and your class have created and share it in a tweet using #UnlockCreativity

---

1. https://www.instructables.com/id/How-to-Make-Plarn-Plastic-Bag-Yarn-For-Knitting-/

RETHINK WHAT'S POSSIBLE

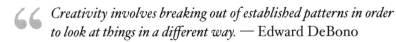
Creativity involves breaking out of established patterns in order to look at things in a different way. — Edward DeBono

CREATIVE TECHNOLOGY IN THE CLASSROOM

When High Tech High founder Larry Rosenstock was given a chance to create a school from scratch, he rose to the challenge by developing one of the most talked-about high schools in the United States. He questioned the traditional structure of school and urged others to rethink what school could be like. Together, he and his team reimagined teaching and learning in a way that broke traditional boundaries and created limitless possibilities for students.

Though the name "High Tech High" contains the word *tech*, the focus in their school is not on technology, but more about developing learners to be creative, reflective thinkers. The educators there have reimagined their teaching practices as well as what it means to use technology as a part of authentic learning. Technology can be a pathway to creativity, but it is one of many. Students can use technology skills to express themselves, demonstrate their passions, and articulate their learning.

As a former elementary principal, I loved walking into our makerspace and talking to the students about what they were working on. It was one of the best parts of the job. Observing student projects as they progressed through different stages was an interesting process. Some students preferred working on messy projects like papier mâché or hands-on tinkering at the sewing machine. Others like building with K'Nex or Legos. Some gravitated to the computers where they tried new programs or researched project ideas.

One morning I walked in and noticed a student sitting alone at the computer. He looked frustrated, tongue out between pursed lips, scrunched eyebrows. When asked to explain what he was working on, he shared that he was using the Scratch program as a part of his "passion project." His 5th-grade class had to choose something they were interested in and pursue that passion every Wednesday afternoon. Passion projects, similar to Genius Hour, are founded on the idea that students can spend time each week working on a topic of their choosing (honoring students voice and choice). He decided that he would teach himself to code and design a digital animation project to share with his class. That afternoon he was due to share his project and wanted to make sure that every component was in perfect working order.

A student who often gravitated towards technology combined his interest in video games with his passion for learning a new skill. Throughout the nine weeks, he watched video tutorials, connected with other "Scratchers" online, and taught himself all the basics. He created characters, designed backgrounds, and ultimately created an entire story around his animation. Proud of the fact that he taught himself how to do it, he now wanted to teach others and even started a student Scratch Club at lunchtime, building a creative network of buddies who decided to learn along with him. He was able to leverage his creativity by using different technology tools to achieve his goal.

Technology doesn't have to mean all the latest devices and expensive equipment. Let's stop and think about this differently. Tech can mean any apps, websites, or other educational tools that can ignite a creative spark in students. From simple to complex, technology can be any tool that helps you accomplish a goal.

The truth is, technology can enhance creativity for some, but may inhibit it for others. It is important to offer a balance of tech and non-tech options in the classroom, especially when it comes to creative tasks. This is an opportunity to include student choice and boost creative agility.

Technology can leverage creativity, as it provides new ways for students to design, build, and make. Technology can offer another way to learn in a hands-on way. Creative tech in the classroom may mean using images, videos, STEM tools, game design, maker technology, blogs, and social media to maximize student creativity. Cameras, iPads, robots, and power tools are all technologies that, in the hands of students, can fuel a creative opportunity. Reimagine these technology tools and the way they can create an impact in the classroom.

NEW OPPORTUNITIES THROUGH TECH

Many of our students enjoy technology. Some may even be hooked—playing video games, connecting with peers online, and creating videos to post on social media. Ironically, many of these students might also claim that they aren't creative. We have an opportunity right now to capitalize on student interest in tech and add a layer of creativity to it.

When we put technology in the hands of our students, we are unlocking creative possibilities for them with the potential to use any tool to maximize their learning. Our students are digital natives. They are already immersed in the fast-paced world of video games, Google searches, and complex "all in one" devices that rest in the palms of their hands. They don't know what it's like to wait until the phone line is free to "dial-up" the world wide web. They probably haven't experienced games like Pong and Space Invaders that moved in slow pixelated patterns. They have always been able to call anyone at any time, find out information in an instant, and create whatever is in their imaginations. Technology can help them do that.

Technology is constantly changing and improving, faster than we can imagine. Keeping up with all the latest and greatest tools is a challenge, but our students are always looking for the next cool tool, game, or device. We can capitalize on this interest and use it to our creative advantage.

I don't know about you, but when I'm not sure how to use a new tech tool, I hand it over to a student. When you can't think of how that new app can enhance instruction, ask your class! If you are struggling with how to fit a new technology experience into your curriculum, your students will know a way.

It's important to remember that technology is a tool that can enhance the learning experience. Students see technology as an opportunity to create. Present students with the concepts or skills they will be learning and then give them the chance to offer a tool to use that would help them learn best.

With all the tech that surrounds them, we want to be able to use it as a tool to meet a larger objective that will lead to creative thinking, rather than have them think the tool or tech is the end game. Every video, every game, and every new tool is an opportunity for students to learn something new and unlock their creativity. Let's reimagine how we might provide creative opportunities using technology as a pathway to unlock student imagination.

CREATIVITY NOTEBOOK

From time to time, I bring home "goodies" from
work. My sons know that I'm an educator and
they love the perks that can sometimes come with
my job.

Whether it's sample books from a publisher or a
"fancy" pen from a conference, my kids know that
they are likely to find something good in my work
bag.

After bringing home a classroom kit of Little Bits,
my boys became fascinated with the way that
technology could make things move, light up, and
make noise.

They tinkered with the different parts, designing
new creations and combining parts of this kit
with Legos and K'Nex from around our house.

They readily looked beyond the directions and
sought out new ways to rethink what was
possible with the materials. I love that sense of
curiosity and discovery that is so innate to
learners at this age. If only we could capture
that and make it multiply throughout our schools.

DIGITAL EXPLORATION

Technology doesn't have to mean a device in hand. When we
reimagine our teaching, educational technology can be anything that
upgrades learning in a new and better way. Interacting with technology

might mean using virtual reality goggles or a robotics kit, but it can also mean a hands-on tool. Consider this example:

A group of young inventors was working with Strawbees, an engineering toy that uses straws and connectors as a flexible building tool. The group was tasked with creating a new game with the materials. Students worked individually and in pairs to sketch a design. They tinkered and prototyped as they tried to manipulate the new material. They used what they knew about three-dimensional shapes to create a tabletop game that included two goals and a catapult-like launcher. They used content knowledge from science about how energy is stored, transferred, and converted along with their background knowledge on tension, force, and gravity to create a working catapult. The Strawbees were new to the students, allowing them to explore in different ways, using the materials to create something unexpected.

Another group of students collaborated to design a maze on the floor with painter's tape. They mapped out a path on paper and then transferred their idea to the tile floor. Their goal was to program a robot that they built to navigate the maze. Students demonstrated their understanding of angles within the maze and block-based coding through their programming, in addition to constructing the robot. Devices in hand, they followed their bot to see if the goal was accomplished or where their program fell short.

Both of these examples use different types of technology. While one was more digital and the other more physical, both tools provided students with exposure to materials that provided open-ended possibilities. Both activities engaged the students in creating something new and using their knowledge from different content areas to problem solve. Reflect on what technology looks like in your classroom and whether it focuses on consumption or creation. Reimagine the use of hands-on tools within the learning environment and find ways to use technology as a pathway to creative expression.

OFFER CHOICES

Technology is one tool of many used to enhance creativity. A student who isn't a strong writer may be a great speaker, able to do the voice-over for a video produced by peers. Another student who may not feel like a great artist can use technology tools to create stunning digital graphics. Sometimes all we need to do to support new learning through technology is provide access to our students. Giving learners access to creative technologies may help them to connect with a tool that will meet their needs and advance their creative thinking.

Your school might already be 1:1, or you may have limited access to technology. Creating a plan to incorporate creative technology into the classroom will be tailored to your needs and the needs of your students. The plan might include a timeline for technology use or topics for personal learning. It's important to write down your plan. This step makes it more concrete and shows some intention on your part to commit it to writing.

Set a personal goal. Write down one commitment that you will make to infuse technology tools into your classroom. The goal might be for you personally or a collective goal that you want to set for your students. When you set goals and work toward them, you are developing creative habits and increasing stamina.

- I will learn one new technology tool this month.
- I will regularly read one educational technology blog.
- Our class will spend one period each quarter exploring new technology and sharing what we've learned with others.
- Our teaching team will have lunch together on the first Friday of every month and talk about the tech tools we are trying in the classroom.

These may sound simple, but our lives as educators can be hectic. Write down your commitment and put it somewhere you will see it and be reminded. When we create a personal goal, it is important to follow it and hold ourselves accountable for both personal and professional growth, especially with so many things pulling us in different directions.

> ## RIGHT NOW, WE HAVE AN OPPORTUNITY TO CAPITALIZE ON STUDENT INTEREST IN TECH AND ADD A LAYER OF CREATIVITY.

WELCOME TO THE TECH LOUNGE

There are so many technology tools out there that it can be a challenge to keep them all straight. Build capacity in your students as tech experts by giving them the opportunity to explore a variety of tools that might meet their creative needs and interests. While the students are certainly coming to school with a great deal of tech knowledge already, we can further support their learning by ensuring that students have the time and access to advance their skills in school.

Establish a time of day or a period within the week for "Tech Lounge." This can be a set time for students to explore different apps or websites, as well as an opportunity for students to collaborate and share knowledge. Dedicate the last period of the day or revise your schedule to create "Techy Tuesdays," or allocate some special time to share that is embedded into a daily class meeting. This might mean that school principals ask teachers to cover the lounge on a rotating basis, offer a stipend, or create a free period for teachers who are willing to step up and support this creative initiative. Find a strategy that will work for your class, and that makes sense within the structure of your school. Here's one way to invite students into the Tech Lounge:

Step 1: Ask students to identify an area of interest:

- Are they designers—students who aspire to create beautiful images or design graphics for a corporation?
- Do you have creative writers—looking to write a novel, intrigued by poetry, or those who want to create the next amazing picture book? Students interested in writing can benefit from tech tools that can enhance their process.
- Who doesn't want to be the next YouTube star? Producers will jump at the chance to create videos or try their skills at music production.
- Want to combine knowledge and work together? Students interested in collaborating will revel in the opportunity to connect with others while creating through the use of classroom tech tools.
- Have any gamers in the class? Creating their own video games combines creative skills with knowledge of programming and design, resulting in student-driven technology projects.

Step 2: Provide time for students to explore tools like these or other new apps and websites that pique their creative interests.

Designers	Writers	Producers	Collaborators	Gamers
Canva	Book Creator *	Garageband	Flipgrid	Game Salad *
Buncee	Storybird	TouchCast	Seesaw	Scratch
Paper 53	Edublogs	HP Reveal	Padlet	Infinite Arcade *
DoInk *	BoomWriter	Powtoon *	Sweet Drawpad	Bloxels *

While most of these are tech tools are free, those requiring a purchase are indicated with an * asterisk.

Step 3: Build in time to reflect on new learnings and share discoveries with the class. This can happen as individuals share out with the group during a discussion, tweet out something new that they learned, or recommend a tech tool to their peers by posting a review on a class bulletin board or website.

Use this grid as a potential template for creative tech choices and add new ones as tools grow and change. This could even be a display in your classroom that students can access and change based on their interests, incorporating more voice and choice within the classroom.

SHOW WHAT YOU KNOW

Students are fascinated by the stories we tell them about our lives. When we make connections with our students, they often become intrigued by the personal experiences we have and the things we know. We can help them reimagine their learning by allowing them to do the same thing when we assess them.

We are all responsible for assessing the learning of our students. Sometimes we do that through online quizzes or through paper and pencil tests. Other times, we have students write reports or respond to questions in a journal. In some classes, students might do a demonstration or a presentation to show what they have learned. Showing what you know can happen through different mediums. Including technology as an option for students to show what they know can have positive outcomes for learners.

Here's how it works:

- Think about the next unit you are teaching. What's the next story in your reading book, the next chapter in the history text, or the next unit in science or math?
- How are you planning to assess this new learning? Whatever your plan is, keep it. Just add one technology-oriented option for your students. Choose one tech alternative that would allow students to infuse some creativity into the assessment while still meeting your expectations for the content.

How might students:

- Create a video to demonstrate their understanding of body systems for physical education and health class?
- Design a digital animation to retell key events in history class?
- Make a 3-D model of a molecule or cell in science class?
- Blog their reaction to a story they read in English Language Arts?
- Produce a newscast sharing a new concept learned in art class?
- Build a video game that doubles as a review of math facts?

Consider posting these options somewhere in your classroom, so students understand that their learning will be measured in a variety of ways. Making these visible in the classroom will also communicate with other teachers, parents, and classroom visitors that creativity is valued in this space. There is a time and a place for traditional assessments, but don't let those stifle the creativity of your students. Provide them with creative options for showing what they know by incorporating technology tools, when possible.

Using technology tools in the classroom also gives students the chance to grow from feedback. Tech enables students to give and receive feedback through blogs and digital portfolios. It facilitates sharing and collaboration through the connected nature of modern technology tools; tools that are changing every day to make us more connected and more collaborative in every way.

SPARK INTEREST THROUGH TECHNOLOGY

We can reimagine our teaching practices through a technology lens, adding options for students that can enhance their creativity. When technology is used strategically, it can unlock creativity and open up possibilities for student learning. Technology is just one tool that can spark interest in students and bring out creative imagination. Don't rely on technology, but find meaningful ways to incorporate it into your classroom. This balance can occur when you introduce a new app to your class or allow video reflection as an assessment option in your class.

CREATIVE CONSIDERATIONS

Thinking differently about our teaching practices requires ongoing reflection. We also need to reevaluate how we frame creativity in our schools. Gamers, animators, and graphic designers possess incredible creative agility. Technology can be used in different ways to leverage student creativity in the classroom. How do you define technology? What tools are considered tech in your district? How might technology empower your students to create in the classroom?

INVITATIONS TO IMAGINATION

Technology is one tool that you can use to unlock creativity for students. Try one of these options that can enhance your instruction and provide a creative outlet for your students.

• Write one creative tech goal for yourself or your class. Set a target and work to meet it.

• Think about the designers, writers, or gamers in your classroom. Schedule time for them to explore tech tools that will help them to express creativity in their own way.

• Add one new tech option to your classroom assessment plan.

• What's your favorite way to leverage creativity in the classroom through the use of technology? Take a picture of students doing that and tweet it out using #UnlockCreativity

NURTURE A COLLABORATIVE CULTURE

 The best collaborations create something bigger than the sum of what each person can create on their own. — Anonymous

DEVELOP LEARNING CONNECTIONS

Picture a patchwork quilt, one that your great grandmother made with dozens of interlocking squares carefully crafted to create a larger masterpiece. Each piece is designed to be beautiful in its own right, but when combined with dozens of others, the single square adds its own unique contribution to the bigger picture.

Now visualize your classroom full of students. As diverse as each quilt square, your students are unique individuals. When pieced together, your individual students make up the culture of your classroom. As lead learners in the classroom, we are the quiltmakers, piecing together all of the parts of our quilt. We have the ability to direct the layout of the quilt and can influence the overall outcome.

We can also create a similar impact on our classroom environment and the culture we foster within that space. If our classroom culture embraces collaboration, it will be evident as learners connect, engage, and discuss their learning. Once established, this culture will support the development of our students as they see their creative contributions as one piece of the classroom quilt. The tone we set and the opportunities we provide show students that our space is welcoming, connected, and creative. The way we design lessons and projects for students that engage them in creative, collaborative groups can create a culture of connectedness in the classroom.

Consider this example of a learning experience for a group of high school students. The students are standing in front of the room, pitching an idea to a panel of community stakeholders. This semester-long project culminated in a multimedia presentation of their research and proposals. They were tasked with coming up with a solution to a problem that their community was facing.

This experiential learning opportunity started with a critical look at their local neighborhoods and delved students into inquiry and critical thinking. Their initial research included collecting observational and interview data. They had to look at multiple sources of information and made decisions about what they discovered. Students organized and interpreted the data, then prepared graphs and charts to represent the information.

Some students took a design approach, creating a physical product or invention to solve their identified problem. These students designed prototypes using cardboard models or used their 3-D printing skills. Other teams of students created informational videos calling attention to their identified issue. One team planned an event at a community park to increase awareness of a problem they discovered. Each team came prepared to share their topic and to convey its importance to their audience. This was an authentic way for students to collaborate on a task that was rooted in their commitment to their community.

Think about all that went into these student presentations. Students used speaking and listening skills. They needed to consider art elements and design in their presentation and their product design. The project required application of knowledge from multiple content areas, coupled with the creativity and perseverance required to accomplish a complex task like this one.

This project didn't transpire overnight. It required intentional steps on the part of the teaching team to equip students in a way that would help them succeed in a project-based task. It is this type of task that students need to collaborate on. When we present students with complex tasks, it encourages them to collaborate with their peers. Since the tasks are often too big for one individual to do on their own, the combined expertise from multiple students can advance the project to new heights.

Collaboration skills can be built through many of the strategies that have been presented throughout this book. When students are presented with engineering and design challenges or STEAM learning opportunities, collaboration skills are critical to the success of these tasks. When students are sharing technology tools or build a creative mindset for making, they are often reflecting with peers and building the relationships necessary for a strong foundation of collaboration.

> BE INTENTIONAL ABOUT DESIGNING THE TYPES OF LEARNING THAT WILL NOT ONLY MEET THE NEEDS OF YOUR STUDENTS, BUT ALSO ENGAGE THEM IN CREATIVE THINKING AND COLLABORATION.

GENERATE COLLECTIVE CREATIVITY

It has been questioned whether creativity is about the individuals or the ideas. When learners gather, ideas are shared. Sometimes those ideas build on one another and evolve into a bigger, better idea. Sometimes the creativity transforms and develops into a new idea. So, is it the idea that has power, or is it the people that ignite the creative spark for that idea to grow?

There is nothing wrong with creativity in isolation. Some of the world's most creative individuals are often thought to have worked best in isolation and solitude. Creativity can be sparked for individual dreamers and wanderers, but there is power in the collective creativity that comes from working with a collaborative team.

Think about how we might set up learning groups within the classroom. We often choose (or even assign) a leader, a recorder, a reporter, or a materials manager. Whatever names you may give to these roles, the idea is the same. We aspire to design well-balanced student groups that allow everyone's strengths to be used for the benefit of the group. As the lead learner in the classroom, we are looking at the creative potential of the group and trying to orchestrate a successful combination of individuals. Sometimes that type of structure is needed to develop a collaborative culture within the classroom. Creative classrooms provide opportunities for students to connect with one another and find common interests through dialogue and active learning tasks. As students develop strong relationships and collaboration skills, they can use that to unlock the collective creativity of the group.

By building trust in the classroom, we can also develop the collective creativity that can advance student learning.

CREATIVITY NOTEBOOK

I admit it. I am guilty of isolating myself and not being open to collaboration. At different times in my career, I have closed myself off to learning and connecting with others.

As a brand new teacher, I was too afraid to put myself out there. I was terrified to be judged by others. I thought if I just closed my door, taught my kids, and kept to myself everything would be just fine.

Boy, was I wrong!

As I started collaborating with other new teachers and some colleagues within my hallway, I began to see all that I was missing. The daily inspiration, smiles, and encouragement allowed me to be better for my students.

The sharing of ideas and visits to other classrooms showed me that there were other ways to accomplish my goals-- better ways.

When I opened my mind and heart up to connect with others, my world changed. My teaching changed for the better.

COLLABORATION BUILDS TRUST

Have you ever presented a group project to your class and just sent them off to complete it? Chances are, without careful consideration and some relationship building, the group work may have fallen flat. In order for students to work cooperatively with others, we must create an atmosphere of trust in the classroom so that groups of different students can work together effectively without our organizational hand in the mix.

Building trust can happen as we expose students to the opinions and perspectives of other students, and by equipping them with the tools to process and respond to those ideas. Trust is built when students rely on the efforts of their classmates to get a job done. Trust is built when we work together on something we feel passionate about. Creative teachers build these opportunities within their classrooms, providing collaborative tasks in which students can learn from one another.

We need to provide opportunities for students to work with diverse people—people outside of their circle of friends and spheres of influence. We need to set them up to learn from one another and recognize the benefits of collaborating with others who may have more or different knowledge than we do. Each individual's strengths and needs are different. It is often through these experiences that students recognize they can create something unbelievable when they collaborate with others.

The culture that you've established in your classroom can promote collaboration or inhibit it, providing both formal and informal ways for students to connect and learn from one another. We can create tasks for students that we know will lead to collaborative discussions. We can facilitate learning opportunities and plan instruction that will require collaborative work. We can also set up conditions in the classroom that will lead to trust-building between students and among groups to engage them in work that will boost the collective creativity of the entire class.

QUADRANT QUERIES

Shared creativity happens when we engage in tasks that challenge our critical thinking and allow us to connect with others. We can provide learning experiences that ensure student dialogue and prompt collaboration.

These tasks might encourage students to ponder a challenging question or consider a new idea. The task might push students to identify a perspective and engage in a debate. The task might also bring students together to align their opinions on a topic.

One strategy that can pull students into collaborative conversations is through Quadrant Queries. This small group strategy can be done in most grade levels and subject areas as a way to get students thinking creatively and to engage them in discussion through writing and drawing.

Here's how to set up this collaborative task:

Step 1: If you are lucky enough to have writable surfaces in your classrooms, great. If not, cover your tables or desks with butcher paper.

Step 2: Draw a circle in the middle of the area and create four quadrants from the remaining space. There are different versions of this activity, but for the purposes of unlocking creativity, we are going to use the following questions which should be written with one in each of the four quadrants.

- What is positive about this idea/question/concept?
- What concerns do I have about this idea/question/concept?
- How might this idea/question/concept impact me?
- Are there possible extensions or alternatives to this idea?

Step 3: Inside the circle, write the creative idea, question, or concept. This is the topic that students will focus on as they engage in the task. It should spark interest, dialogue, and may even trigger a debate. It might be something related to curricular content, current events, or something directly related to school. Here are a few examples:

- A community concert is scheduled at the park next Friday.
- Recess time is changing from after lunch to before lunch.
- More electives need to be offered at school.
- Students can start bringing pets to school.
- Food trucks are going to be available at football games.
- School bathrooms will be painted with student murals.

Step 4: Divide the students into groups of four and assign each individual to one quadrant as a starting point.

Step 5: Determine a set time for the task. Usually 15-20 minutes is adequate when you are trying this for the first time. Two minutes will be spent in each quadrant.

Step 6: Students will move to each quadrant rotating every two minutes. During their time in each space, they will use the prompt or question you provided to write or draw a response to the topic in the center circle. Once students move to another quadrant, they will have their own ideas to include, but will also have the chance to review responses from their team members.

Step 7: Once all of the students have moved through each quadrant, take the last two minutes for students to go back and reread or respond to any comments they have missed.

Step 8: Each group will spend the remaining minutes in discussion, summarizing their thoughts and asking each other clarifying questions about what was written or drawn.

This strategy will prompt student thinking about different topics but also engage them in discussion. It can be a springboard for new projects, an introduction to class debates, or it can simply be a way to build teamwork within your classes. The practice of working with different table groups and rotating through the quadrants can help students increase their communication skills, both written and verbal, as well as interpersonal skills. This activity and others that support collaboration skills help to build a sense of community in the classroom; a creative community of collaborative learners.

PROJECT-BASED LEARNING

The story that opened this chapter provides one example of the possible creative outcomes that occur when students engage in project-based learning. One strategy for increasing collaborative creativity is through project-based learning experiences (PBLs). Similar in some ways to problem-based learning (also known as PBL), this instructional approach has some different features than the strategy with the same acronym. Project-based learning often encompasses multiple content areas, whereas problem-based learning may be zeroed in on just math or science. Project-based learning culminates with a project, presentation, or performance. Problem-based learning ends with a solution that can be communicated through speaking or writing as opposed to an integrated project. It is an instructional strategy that often extends for several weeks or longer and provides an integrated approach combining multiple subject areas into a topic of study. Through questions and collaborative research, students engaging in PBL can expand their creativity. PBLs can solve problems, educate the community, and even persuade others to act.

Project-based learning doesn't mean that we just create projects for students to engage in. True project-based learning is driven by the idea of creating change and making a difference. This can happen when students:

- Raise awareness around a topic.
- Call others to action.
- Solve a community problem.
- Design a better process.

Project-based learning can result in an unlimited number of outcomes, which is the part that empowers our students and terrifies teachers. PBL isn't measured with a quiz or a research report. It doesn't fit nicely into a gradebook. It can get messy, but remember messy learning is good learning! PBL isn't something that you can plan too far in advance, and you certainly can't use last year's lesson plans. It is driven by the needs and interests of the learners—not by teacher convenience.

Steve Jobs said, "We are here to put a dent in the universe. Otherwise, why else even be here?" That's exactly what PBL can do when we give students voice and choice. They get to choose a place to make their dent. They decide how they will make their mark in this learning journey. It is not prescribed. It is not in the manual. It is the path that students choose to pursue as a collective group of creative thinkers and problem solvers.

It all starts with a driving question. A driving question is meant to serve as an overarching guide to student learning. These are big questions that are not easy to answer and usually lead to even more questions. Driving questions might be provocative and arise from real-world situations. They can build from student or community issues or can be at the heart of the content in your course. Here are some examples of open-ended driving questions.

How might we:

- Create a more sustainable environment in our neighborhood?
- Teach others about the benefits of bees?
- Design a safer school environment?
- Increase awareness of the rise in addiction-related crimes in the community?

Project-based learning is an opportunity for students to work collaboratively to investigate a topic and dive into some deep thinking. It involves exploration, research, writing, and thinking. Work through project-based learning can include conducting interviews, watching videos, and doing fieldwork. It is a method for students to dig deeply into a topic, exploring multiple topics stemming from the driving question. As students learn new information, they are thinking about ways to share that information with others. The outcome of project-based learning experiences usually culminates in public sharing through exhibitions, presentations, or public service announcements. The way students share the potential answers to their driving questions opens up many creative possibilities.

Project-based learning can be a meaningful way for students to not only to build collaboration skills, but also to strengthen their creative agility while developing empathy for others through innovation and design. It presents the opportunity for students to see if their learning "makes a dent" in their original problem or issue. When they do make a dent, it is powerful for students that their creative efforts have reached others and made a difference in their school, community, or region.

FIND YOUR CREATIVE CREW

Collaboration isn't just important for your students. It is also critical for your creative development. We talked about ways to develop your creative agility by establishing creative habits and sharing your stories with others, but how will you sustain your creative inspiration over time?

Finding your creative crew can provide much-needed encouragement and creative inspiration when you're out of fuel. You may need some support on your creative journey, to connect with other educators and find a crew of those pursuing similar interests. Your creative crew will help hold you accountable as you commit to this creative journey. Some call it a professional learning network (PLN), and some call it a personal learning family (PLF). Whatever name you give it, this is your group of people who will provide support and share their creative energy whenever you need it most. Take these steps to build your creative crew:

1. If you're not on social media, what are you waiting for? Twitter, Facebook, and Instagram are all ways to connect with creative educators and join a community that supports you.
2. Join in a Twitter chat to find new tools and see some creativity in action. Check out #dtk12chat, #CreateEDU and #STEAMMakerChat.
3. Connect with creative individuals who are sharing innovative practices on Twitter. Creative classroom teachers, future-ready librarians, and forward-thinking school leaders can provide creative inspiration. Follow creative educators like @FugleFun, @garymdonahue, and @ReneeWellsSTEAM.
4. Check out Instagram and follow creative thinkers like @artsmartnynj or @TheMerrillsEDU. Whether you are interested in digital tools or colorful artistic expression, there are tons of creatives to connect with.

5. Find a creative group to join on Facebook or explore new ideas on message boards like https://teachers.net/. There are so many ways to find "your people," choose whatever way works best for you!

Social media is a powerful way to expand your knowledge base and become a part of a larger creative movement. Find your crew, and it will not only benefit your own personal growth, but will also likely influence the learning and creativity of the students you teach!

SEEK OUT WAYS TO COLLABORATE

While some have argued that collaboration kills creativity, this chapter has provided some powerful examples of how creativity can thrive through collaboration with others. Collaboration can be a way to spark our creativity through dialogue and reflection and even call students to action. When a group of students is engaged in creative collaboration, the collective knowledge and creative energy can propel students into new ideas and experiences.

Collaboration builds the skills that students will need to succeed in the future and establishes a classroom culture that values the contributions of others. Students will likely work on teams with people who come from different backgrounds and bring different skill sets to the table. When we provide opportunities for collaboration in the classroom, we are unlocking their creative potential and also preparing them for the future.

CREATIVE CONSIDERATIONS

A collaborative culture is created in the classroom as we design opportunities for students that build individual and collective creativity. We can set up students to experience the power of collaboration as they connect with their peers and their community. A collaborative culture supports the learning and development of your students and you.

Developing a collaborative spirit in the classroom takes time, but we can take steps to build a culture that connects students with one another while also connecting them to creative content. Do students feel a sense of collaborative culture in your classroom? How will you know? How might you set up the conditions to promote collective creativity through collaboration in your classroom?

INVITATIONS TO IMAGINATION

A collaborative culture is critical in the classroom. It supports the development of students as they build communication and creation skills. Take a step in your creative growth and unleash one of these strategies to embrace a creative culture in your school.

• Investigate project-based learning as a way to engage students in authentic learning.

• Plan a collaborative project by building bridges across classrooms through peer mentoring.

• Build your personal crew of creative collaborators by following five new creative thinkers on social media this week.

• Who are your best collaborators? Call out their creativity on social media. Tweet it out using #UnlockCreativity

EXTEND THE LEARNING

 Creativity is just connecting things. — Steve Jobs

BEYOND THE BOUNDARIES

The library was filled with classes of sixth graders, but you could hear a pin drop. The students were sitting quietly as they listened to a guest speaker from Animal Friends, a local shelter for dogs, cats, and other animals. The speaker had a dog with her, that sat on the floor playing with some toys the handler brought. The students heard about some of the statistics for the shelter, the number of animals they support and the amount of food and items the animals need. As they developed their understanding, students realized that there was a need at the shelter, not only for volunteers and supplies, but also for things that the students might be able to contribute.

As the students listened, you could almost see their empathy building. They were drawn to the stories of the animals in the shelter. They loved the shelter ambassador who came to visit and expressed concerns about the needs of the animals. This empathy propelled them into action. The speaker continued with her presentation and began to show students things they could create that would contribute to the shelter.

Students were intrigued when the speaker began to share things they could make from everyday items and supplies. Catnip pillows sewn with fabric squares and some thread could be made easily in our makerspace with the purchase of some cat treats. Simple cat toys that are great for pawing and scratching could be made out of recycled egg cartons and pipe cleaners. Students could use toilet paper rolls to create dog treats to keep dogs busy at the shelter. No-sew fleece blankets could also be made for dogs to keep them feeling cozy. Students had no idea that there were so many ways they could use their creativity to make a difference.

The students were motivated to use their creativity in a meaningful way that extended their reach beyond the classroom space. They had a dozen ideas for creating safe toys and accessories for shelter animals. Student teams focused on their projects at school, but many also worked on them at home. Some students even brought in materials and collected donations from their families and friends.

Once all of the pet toys and other items were made, students took a trip to the shelter to present their donations. This opportunity to work creatively for the benefit of others built students' understanding and empathy while also building collaboration and communication skills. Infusing creativity into the project helped students activate their creative agility to think about possible solutions for a real-world problem in their community.

Listening to an inspirational speaker or reading a powerful book can propel you into action. A great song or a peaceful view can motivate you to make a difference. Hearing a good story may compel you to make a change. As adults, we experience this feeling in a lot of different ways, but it may not be the same for our students. We can create opportunities that will inspire them into action and extend their learning beyond the boundaries of the classroom.

Extending the learning beyond the classroom walls shows students their voice matters, and their work has value. If we make time and space for creative thinking and imagination, but it stays confined within your classroom, what message is that sending your students? "OK, your creation is good. We had fun being creative. Now let's put that aside and get back to the real work." When you unlock creativity in your classroom, it is only the beginning of the potential learning you can share with your students. Creativity is magnified when it is shared!

EXTENDING THE LEARNING BEYOND THE CLASSROOM WALLS SHOWS STUDENTS THEIR VOICE MATTERS AND THEIR WORK HAS VALUE.

REAL-WORLD APPLICATION

Sometimes the phrase "real-world" can be overused in education. It has become somewhat of a buzzword, but real-world opportunities for students are critical to their learning and development. What we really mean when we say real-world is meaningful learning that is connected to an authentic audience. It refers to the learning that applies to potential jobs of the future and conversations with experts in the field. These are all important components of real-world applications that we can develop within our classrooms.

Real-world not only means building the skills that our students will likely need beyond their K-12 education, but also fostering the skills that are needed right now. It means engaging in experiences that are authentic and not created solely for the purpose of school. Sometimes it means using realistic tools of the workplace and interacting with experts in the field—doing the work of "real" people.

We can create learning conditions that put students into these authentic learning experiences. Creative educators can establish connections between our work in the classroom with the work that happens outside of the classroom. This is real.

Real-world work requires creativity. It requires that people are thinking about and exploring solutions to complex problems. This is the work that our students will engage in when they leave our class-rooms. We can use content connections in the classroom and align them to the work of creative experts in the field. By doing this, we can give our students a glimpse into creative careers. Exposing students to authentic creative problem-solving is one way to increase their creative agility and show students that what they are learning in the classroom matters and can have a direct connection to creative work in the real world.

NETWORK OF LEARNERS

As we expanded our personal network in the last chapter, we will grow that network for our students so that we are equipped to extend learning beyond the traditional classroom boundaries. You can't extend learning beyond the boundaries of your classroom if you aren't a connected educator. Being connected is important, as it offers educa-tors the chance to build supportive relationships and productive part-ners in the work we do. It allows us to reach beyond our schools and communities and connect with other creative individuals across the globe. When we begin to grow our network of support, we often grow personally as individuals. Our learning network helps to push our thinking, helping us to become stronger and often more creative class-room teachers.

A professional learning network is a group of educators supporting one another's efforts to improve teaching and learning. Sometimes learning networks are developed within schools and districts through face-to-face interactions. These might be in the form of book study groups or learning communities pursuing a topic of interest. In the current tech-nology age, our professional learning networks might include people that we've never even met. Social media allows us to establish a creative network of support with people all over the world. This network might include educators, school leaders, authors, artists, and CEOs.

When we have a network to lean on, it makes our job as creative educators just a little bit easier. If you have an idea you aren't sure about, reach out to your network. When you are looking for classroom resources, someone within your network will be able to provide some guidance. As you plan for a creative project, your network may provide support that transforms your instruction or uplifts the work of your students in amazing ways.

While you are working to build your learning network, you can expand it by connecting with other educators who are reading this book by using the hashtag #UnlockCreativity or doing a book study. It is also important to build a network of support for your students.

STEPS TO CONNECT CREATIVE LEARNING

As we establish creative learning experiences for students within our classrooms, we can extend that learning beyond our typical reach— making connections to college, career, and beyond. Employers want graduates who are creative, confident, and collaborative. Our students want daily opportunities to engage in relevant learning experiences. Potential employers in the real world want employees who can work effectively as a team and prioritize their work. They want clear communicators who make decisions and process information in the workplace.

In creative classrooms, we can take steps to develop learning experiences that will develop future-ready skills in our students. Don't implement a creative project just because you feel like you have to.

- Make it relevant.
- Connect it to something students are interested in.
- Align the work to the curriculum.
- Create learning that reflects the careers of creative thinkers.

When we extend the learning to go above and beyond the curriculum itself, we open doors to creativity within every student. Tapping into their interests and showing them relevancy to their lives can change how they view their education. Let's design some creative opportunities to extend creative learning beyond the classroom.

STEP INTO THE SHARK TANK

When students develop a creative mindset, some create to express themselves or use creativity as a way to solve problems. Some unlock their creative mindset and use it as a means to design and invent new products. No doubt you've watched an episode or two of the TV show *Shark Tank*. Entrepreneurs take their shot, pitching their creative ideas to financial backers and marketing superstars. From a new tool to make family camping easier or a unique way to clean the bathroom, the sharks hear the creative inventions from hopeful innovators ready to make their creative dreams a reality. You can unlock this same opportunity for students by bringing the shark tank in your classroom.

Here are three simple steps to try this idea in your classroom.

Step 1: Create

- Students brainstorm, design, and prototype an invention.

Step 2: Market

- Create a commercial, website, or other tool to show why your invention is needed.

Step 3: Pitch

- Present your ideas to the sharks in a creative way that gets your message across and makes them want to invest in you.

Tap into your creative network to bring in experts for your shark panel. Think about the creative jobs that the parents of your students might have. Do you know any community members who might be able to volunteer as a shark? Small business owners, engineers, real estate agents—all of these individuals have the creative capacity to support your students and provide them with feedback to succeed in the entrepreneurial world.

One middle school decided to take a swim with the sharks. Teams of students created, marketed, and pitched their ideas to an expert panel. Students came with viable prototypes, creative commercials, and even catchy jingles. A backpack umbrella, a contraption to hold and dispose of tissues in the classroom, or a fidget spinner phone case—the students stretched their imaginations to come up with innovative products to market to their peers.

This creative experience can connect to different content areas within your curriculum. Students research their potential products and size up their competition, building their technology and research skills. As students develop their marketing plan and presentation, they are working on persuasive writing techniques. When students are thinking about advertising and sales, they are not only developing creativity skills, but also building their knowledge in entrepreneurship. Gearing up for a formal presentation, students are further developing their speaking and listening skills, areas that are likely within your state standards.

If the shark tank isn't for you, try another student-focused entrepreneurial project like a lemonade stand or other small business that your class can design, market, and run within your school. One creative twist for the fall or winter months is to set up a hot chocolate stand. Student teams can design their own unique recipes (our middle school teams created chocolate cheesecake, peppermint chocolate, and smores). The team that earned the most money won a special catered lunch. The proceeds from all teams were donated to a local food bank.

Each design team experimented with their recipes, advertised, and sold their creations in the cafeteria at lunchtime for a week. Creating different iterations with ingredients, advertising products, and engaging in a sale provided opportunities for students to tap into knowledge from multiple subject areas. As educators, we can connect this creative learning with standards within science, art, language arts, and math.

Not every child wants to be an inventor or an entrepreneur, but this type of experience allows students to learn about all that it takes to bring a product to consumers. Not every child will like to design and create prototypes, but one student will find this to be their strength. Not every student will excel at marketing, but one student will realize they are really good at it. Not everyone will be effective at delivering the pitch, but one student will find that this is their gift. Multi-layered projects like these provide opportunities to show creativity in different ways, offering creative pathways for students to explore that extends the learning beyond one class period.

EXPAND A CREATIVE NETWORK FOR STUDENTS

In order to connect your students with opportunities beyond the school walls, you will need to develop a network of creative individuals to support the work of your students. Think about the people who are within your existing school network. This might include educators, parents who work in a creative career, or talented community members. This local network can leverage new learning for students and provide opportunities for mentorships that support creative thinking.

If your creative network isn't as robust as you might want, here are a few steps you can take:

- Build a local creative network to support your students. This network should include individuals that can help you to extend creative opportunities beyond the classroom.
- Create a list of the potential connections that could extend learning beyond the classroom walls.
- Small business owners
- Local corporations
- Public libraries

- Community workers (police, fire, medic rescue)
- Create a database of creative mentors who can serve as role models for students.
- Brainstorm a list of skills, careers, or talents that might be beneficial in building the creative confidence of your students (and you!)
- Local artists and musicians
- Architects
- Interior designers
- Landscapers

Add other creative careers to this list that you believe can have a positive impact on your students. This might include local or regional "celebrities" in creative roles that students may admire. Their creative talents might not be what they are best known for, but this will allow students to see the diverse abilities of individuals and the way that creativity can be developed in their community.

CREATIVE CAREER CONNECTIONS

Connecting with experts in the field provides career direction for young innovators. It provides creative inspiration for young students who are developing their craft. For older students, it might put them on a career path to creativity.

What else?

- Coordinate time with creative professionals.
- Plan studio time with artists and designers.
- Arrange workshop time with writers and carpenters.
- Schedule gallery time for sculptors and painters.
- Connect through career talks.
- Ask professionals to give students the inside scoop on their creative careers.
- Have a Google Hangout with a construction manager who can walk your class through a project in process.

- Skype with an illustrator who can talk about their creative process, show you their sketches, or even make one live.
- Plan a field trip (physical or virtual) to a tech startup, a retail store, or a factory and ask professionals how they use creative thinking and problem-solving in their work.
- Engage in exhibitions and celebrations of authentic creative expression.
- Visit the museum, art gallery, or creative studio.
- Attend plays, performances, or local shows.

Connecting students to these potential career pathways will give them the chance to explore future possibilities. Once you've established these connections to careers, use this to extend learning for students. Don't let these experiences be a one-time event. Follow up with ongoing opportunities to reconnect with individuals and revisit topics that resonated with your students. Expand on what students have seen, heard, and experienced by extending the learning.

THE POTENTIAL OF CONNECTED EXPERIENCES

Connected learning occurs at several different levels. It happens when we create learning opportunities for our students that not only connect to content in meaningful ways, but also when we connect students to creative supports in their community. To make this happen, we need to be connected educators, ready to call on our network to boost the learning of our students. It also means connecting within our school community so students can see how the power of connections can unlock new and exciting opportunities to learn, collaborate, and create.

CREATIVE CONSIDERATIONS

Consider the areas within your curriculum that already extend beyond the traditional boundaries of school. Strengthen those connections and unlock new opportunities to amplify creativity— either by bringing more creativity into your classroom or by compelling students to think about creating an impact outside of the classroom. How do you provide students with connected learning opportunities throughout their K-12 education? How do we extend student learning beyond the school day and beyond the school walls?

INVITATIONS TO IMAGINATION

Opportunities exist all around us to provide a creative spark for students and extend the learning beyond the classroom. Look for places where you can develop learning experiences that connect subjects together and creates an impact outside of the school.
• Design an entrepreneurial challenge for students that extends their learning beyond the classroom.
• Expand your network of creative adults that can support you and the work of your students by researching career connections.   Add to your growing list of new ideas.
• Establish one new relationship that will connect your students to creative professionals. Think locally and globally!
• How are you extending learning beyond the classroom walls? Give a shout out to a community partner who has supported the development of student creativity in your classroom!

FINDING YOUR WAY

 Plant an idea in the mind and watch it grow into a tree.

But plant an idea in the heart and a forest it shall be.

— Kenneth Kit Lamug

INNOVATION ACROSS THE CURRICULUM

Picture a traveler heading out on a cross-country trek. Equipped with his backpack full of necessities and map in hand, he heads off on the trail to begin his adventure. The traveler will likely stumble along the way and discover new things. He will bring his knowledge of the road but will also build his knowledge throughout the experience.

On his way to reaching his final destination, the traveler stops to look at interesting sites. He stops and talks with different people along the way. He uses the tools at his disposal to persevere throughout his journey, but it is the connections he makes with other travelers that will stick with him. Though he set out on a journey with an original plan, he may veer from that plan and adjust, just as we do in the classroom.

Creativity is everywhere, sometimes you just need to go and look for it. As you continue your personal journey to unlock creativity within yourself and your students, take a moment to explore the creativity that may be happening around you. A quick walk down the hall might reveal some creative examples that you never noticed before.

Learning walks can take you on a journey without ever leaving your school. Head out on a mission to find pockets of creativity, sparks of innovative thinking, and new ideas in familiar places. As educators, we spend a lot of our time in isolation. We stay in our classrooms, teach our students, attend meetings, and stay to ourselves. As teachers and leaders, we need to be intentional about getting out of the classroom and seeing the curriculum connections that are unlocking creativity in around the school.

Travel to a math class and witness a different approach to learning, or travel to a history class and explore ancient times through a different lens. The key is to travel the hallways with an open mind and be willing to embrace different ways of thinking along the way to spark your own creativity.

As you find your way on this creative journey, your travels may take you in different directions. You will connect with other educators who are also on a similar journey. Collaborate with others and make connections that will nudge your students on their creative journey. Look in unexpected places for creative twists. Search for unconventional approaches within the curriculum. When we do this, the curriculum becomes a tool to draw students in, not silo their learning into predetermined courses.

It takes time to develop connections throughout the curriculum, time for teachers to collaborate and share ideas, Time for teachers to find and vet resources. It takes time to just think about the ways teachers can infuse creativity into the work they are doing. We need to take a creative approach to find time within our already busy schedules to develop curriculum connections that will support the growth of creativity in the classroom.

COLLABORATE ALONG THE WAY

As we are finding our way in this creative journey, we may need the assistance of others just like the traveler who needs guidance out on the trail. Collaborative support from those around us may provide the encouragement we need to take that creative risk or the gentle push to design an unconventional lesson. Finding connections across the curriculum can be a shared task among you and your colleagues. While you can plan effectively in isolation, you may find it beneficial to bounce creative ideas off of your colleagues, even if time to plan cross-curricular lessons may be hard to come by.

If we believe that integrating subject areas within our lessons will provide a richer learning experience for our students, then we need to connect with other educators who are teaching those subjects. This might mean picking the brain of your social studies colleague to get their perspective on an upcoming lesson. It can happen in the way that you connect your third-grade class to the other across the hall for a combined lesson on math and science. Perhaps, you can find an opportunity for a music teacher and a physical education teacher to connect around ideas on music and movement, designing a lesson that honors the content from both subject areas. The possibilities for collaboration are endless when we take time to nurture the connected nature of learning.

Collaboration time allows teachers to find creative connections across their courses. It promotes valuable dialogue across subject areas and grade levels, establishing connections that might not have otherwise been brought to the surface. It is through teacher collaboration and sharing that in turn, new ideas can blossom. This is not to say that creativity can't happen without collaboration, but it can be amplified when we enjoy the benefits of the collective creativity of the group in which we surround ourselves as educators. We can set up these same conditions for our students as they engage in collaboration and build collective creativity in the classroom, sharing their individual expertise with others and magnifying the creative opportunities to connect with others.

CREATIVITY NOTEBOOK

When my son Caden was little, we would often go on walks to look for "treasures," an acorn on the sidewalk or a leaf that found its way to the ground. We would walk in our neighborhood, always on the hunt for something special.

Sometimes we would head home with our pockets full of treasures. We would lay everything out on the dining room table and marvel at what we found.

Maybe we'd break open the acorn or do a leaf rubbing with paper and crayons. Other times we would glue our treasures onto a poster and hang it up in the kitchen.

Sometimes the treasures would disappear only to be found in my son's bedroom on a special shelf where he kept other curious things.

He still notices the little things. He wonders about them. He creates new ideas from known things. That creative spark is always inside him ready to be unleashed.

ESTABLISH LEARNING CONNECTIONS

Why is it that when we think of creativity in schools, we generally think of the arts? Painting, music, drama—those are the creative areas. Maybe your personal image of creativity expands beyond those.

Creativity and innovation are present in much of what we do outside of school, but yet we put limits on creativity inside school.

Students need to see the connections between what they learn in math and how that applies to science. They need to understand that events in history impact the literature we read. They also need to experience creativity beyond their traditional art and music classes. We need to be intentional about showing students the interconnected nature of learning. We can no longer limit their ability to be creative to just a few classes. Creativity is a part of what we all do—in every course, every classroom, every day.

Connecting learning experiences for students provides that a-ha moment when students recognize the math behind artistic elements. It happens when they discover the similarities between poetry and music, or when they see the meaning behind learning science because it will benefit their project in the makerspace. There are so many intersections where critical content knowledge meets hands-on application that we may need help finding our way through the planning, connecting, and designing of creative learning experiences.

Powerful learning occurs when we take the time to design lessons that connect curriculum content, but also when students can connect with others through the content. There are strategies to unravel that will support your ability to create curriculum connections through your own personal development. There are also strategies that support the collaborative connections that can be made for students.

FIND THE TIME

When you find your way, creativity and innovation are possible in any content, subject area, or grade level. What it looks like in social studies, physical education, business courses, math, or foreign language may vary. Teachers can unlock creativity through the way content is introduced, the way lessons are planned and implemented, and the way student learning is assessed.

Time is one of the biggest needs we have in education. We need more time during the school day to connect with our kids. We need more time to instruct critical content in our curriculum. We need more time to plan engaging lessons for our students and more time to collaborate with our colleagues on cross-curricular opportunities.

A great thing happens when we devote the time needed to improve our practice. As we carve out time to investigate curricular connections and have conversations with our colleagues, we will begin to find our way. In turn, this pathway will create more engaging and imaginative learning opportunities for our students.

> CREATIVITY IS A PART OF WHAT WE DO IN EVERY COURSE, EVERY CLASSROOM, EVERY DAY.

TRY A PINEAPPLE CHART

Finding your way may be easier when you have others to join you on the journey. Connect with your colleagues to expand your creativity and learn from others. Sometimes the best professional development you can find is the person right down the hall. Depending on whether you work in a large school or a small school, it may be difficult to know all the great things happening across your building. If you are on a mission to connect with teachers across the curriculum, a pineapple chart (Gonzalez, 2016) might be one option that your school can explore as a tool to share creative ideas and foster cross-curricular collaboration.

The pineapple is known as a symbol of welcome, which is why we often see pineapples on welcome mats or on door decorations in people's homes. It is meant to convey a friendly message that everyone is welcome in the space. So, imagine if we used this universal welcoming sign in our classrooms.

A pineapple chart is one way that we can let others know we welcome them as visitors into our learning space. Pineapple charts are often posted in the main office or some other central location in a school so that everyone can see it. Pineapple charts can look like a grid or matrix that mirrors the times/periods of the school schedule. Here's how it works:

- The blank chart (scheduling grid) is put in a spot where teachers can view it each day.
- Teachers who want to invite others into their classroom can write on the chart by including the time, location, and lesson that they are sharing. For example, Mr. Smith writes his name in a block from 9:45-10:30 in Room 325 to let his colleagues know that he is teaching a creative science lesson that will feature a new app his students are using.
- Other teachers can view the chart (including Mr. Smith's open invitation to his room) and plan to visit a colleague. They can also add their own invitation to the board.
- Sometimes you might happen to be free at the same time your colleague is offering to share a lesson, but we know that doesn't always happen. Ask your school leader for support to see if they can arrange the opportunity for you to visit.

The pineapple chart might be a structure that works for your school, or maybe you have another system to connect with your colleagues throughout the school day. Many teachers use the hashtag #ObserveMe (Kaplinsky, 2016) by posting a sign outside their door to let others know visitors are welcome. The #ObserveMe movement is a way to share the teaching and learning happening in your class with others. It can be a chance to try out a new creative idea or showcase the innovative thinking of your students. When we connect with our colleagues and visit their classrooms, we increase our awareness of the connections between our content and the content of our peers. We seek out ways that our curriculum intersects, across grades and subject areas, and we use the classroom visit as a springboard to future collaborative lessons together.

MAKE CREATIVE MUSIC TOGETHER

As we find our way, we are always looking for guideposts to will help us to find our bearings. When we identify a place where our curriculum connects with others, we have to capitalize on that opportunity. Each connection we make may help us spark a creative idea within our students while also building curricular connections with our colleagues. Take the time to build a creative lesson that connects with another grade level or with a teacher of special subjects. Not only will you model positive communication and collaboration skills for your students, but you will also show students new pathways where creative learning can take them. There are ways we can figuratively and literally make beautiful music together through our instructional design.

If you haven't watched the video of the Landfill Harmonic, this is a must-see for those on this creative journey. It is an amazing story of a man in a small South American town who uses his circumstances to his advantage. Using garbage from the landfill outside his home, he builds musical instruments for kids in the community. Violins, cellos, and drums—his creations are pretty impressive. If that's not enough, he teaches the kids from the community to play the instruments, as well. Their work has taken them all the way to Carnegie Hall to perform. When you step back and look at these instruments, it is crazy to think that everything was made from garbage.

If you have musically inclined students or others who are interested in building and design, dedicate time for your students craft their own musical instruments. Finding your way through a creative project like this one requires both collaboration and curricular connections. One music teacher took advantage of this opportunity and created instruments from recycled materials. Bucket drums, maracas, tambourines, and even some stringed instruments were crafted from materials in the school makerspace. She connected her music content to a story that students were reading in an English Language Arts class so students could deepen their understanding.

Continuing on this journey, the ELA teacher shared the idea with another teacher who had taken an African Drumming class. He offered his skills and shared what he learned with the students. That prompted him to reach out to the social studies teacher who shared some geographic and cultural feedback on the project. If that wasn't enough, the physical education teacher who was already planning for classes to create their own cardio videos, suggested that the students use the drumming in combination with exercise and movement to create videos that would be shared through the school's morning announcements.

This interwoven unit of study was triggered because one teacher watched a video that inspired her to make instruments with her students. Little did she realize that through her connections with other teachers in her building, students would be immersed in a cultural, connected, creative opportunity that stretched far beyond the boundaries of traditional subject area instruction. As this teacher was finding her way, the collaboration from her colleagues served as a support system and led her to deeper learning connections for her students.

Sometimes establishing connections extends beyond instruction and creates bonds between learners, in addition to the connectedness of the content. Let's consider a strategy that will connect students in a powerful way while also building a creative mindset.

CREATIVE COMPANIONS

Finding your way means that you will need a creative network of support, and so will your students. Having a companion on the journey always seems to make things go more smoothly. When we have the chance to collaborate and connect with others, often creativity can be magnified.

We can also provide opportunities for students to work with others and share in learning across the curriculum. Think about ways we connect learners of different ages together through buddy programs and mentorship opportunities. How can we pair students to work together to advance their creative thinking?

"Creative companions" can be used like a buddy program that pairs up older students with younger students. You may have used a strategy like this to create reading buddies, as older students can support the literacy development of their younger buddies. Buddy programs can support reading fluency as younger students read aloud to their buddy. It can also simply promote the joy of reading as an older buddy reads aloud an engaging text to their younger pal.

Let's take this idea and add a creative twist. Creative companions can be set up between different grade levels with a focus on developing creative agility for both members of the pairing. Maybe you are a first-grade teacher and you pair up with a fifth-grade teacher in your building. Maybe you're a high school English teacher, and you connect with a class of fourth graders in another building.

- Establish your pairings before the first activity with your creative companions.
- Buddies can send each other a written note, a picture, or even a video introducing themselves.
- Design an activity with your co-teacher that student pairs can do together, or older students can design a creative activity for their younger buddies that stretches across the curriculum.
- Plan a creative "play date" where the students can get together and do something fun:
- Draw with sidewalk chalk to beautify the school grounds.
- Make a holiday decoration together.
- Build with an educational toy like Strawbees, Brackitz, or K'Nex.
- Get messy with finger paint or clay.
- Can't plan for face-to-face meetings with your Creative Companions? Make it a virtual partnership.
- Connect classes together through Zoom or Google Hangouts.

- Virtual buddies could make Flipgrid videos to share with each other.

Set a goal to bring your students together within the next month. Moving forward, create a schedule that meets your needs, and fits within the time and resources available to you. The younger students will appreciate the mentorship from the older students. The older students might rekindle their interest in childhood creative tasks when they connect with their younger buddies.

CREATIVITY IN UNEXPECTED PLACES

Finding your way through the possible connections in the curriculum will allow you to unleash the creative potential within yourself as you develop instructional strategies that demonstrate interconnected experiences for students. Collaborating with teachers from other departments will expand collective creativity and help you to identify creative paths for students. With so many ways you can connect your instruction to other subject areas, you will need to dedicate time to pursue this important work. Find curriculum connections that will enhance your content as well as offer opportunities for students to collaborate, create, and connect with others.

CREATIVE CONSIDERATIONS

Creativity isn't just for classes in the art department, though they can be a great collaborative resource. There are ways to connect across the curriculum to develop creative opportunities for students. Every classroom can find small ways to add a boost of creativity to their content, instruction, and assessment. What creative connections are you planning to seek out? How will you break down barriers between subject areas to unlock creativity? Who can support you as you find your way?

INVITATIONS TO IMAGINATION

By developing a collaborative spirit and making curricular connections, you can begin to find your way on this creative journey. Identify one strategy that you can begin to implement this week on your road to creativity.

• Get creative about connecting with your colleagues and try a pineapple chart.

• Pair students up to unleash possibilities through a peer buddy program with a focus on building creative thinking.

• Design a lesson with a colleague that crosses the traditional boundaries of your course or subject area.

• What is an upcoming topic in your curriculum? Think about a way that you will establish a creative connection across the curriculum. Share your lesson idea with the #UnlockCreativity community.

EMBRACE CREATIVE STRUGGLE

You can't use up creativity. The more you use, the more you have.
— Maya Angelou

OVERCOME OBSTACLES

Her idea started as a series of scribbles on some dinner napkins. Some were balled up and tossed aside, while others made it into the purse of J.K Rowling and were later added into her notes at home. She toyed with her now well-known stories for years before they even made it into a formal manuscript. She wrote for some time and then frustratedly abandoned the idea altogether before returning to it again years later.

Twelve publishers quickly rejected her first proposal. She could've easily taken this as a sign that she should give up on this creative endeavor, but she kept returning to the ideas that she started with. The heart of this story was a passion for Rowling, so despite ongoing roadblocks and moments of creative struggle, she persevered.

As learners and individuals working to build our creative stamina and agility, we will struggle throughout our creative journey, as will our students. It is what we do in response to that feeling of struggle that will determine our success. Just as Rowling could've turned her back on her creative project, we may want to do the same at times. We can make internal adjustments and look for encouragement to continue on in the face of a creative struggle.

At a recent teacher workshop, tables were covered by white butcher paper along with a centerpiece including some random items: Legos, Play-Doh, beads, string, pipe cleaners, wooden blocks, crayons, and markers. As the teachers entered the room, many were drawn to the creative items and began tinkering. One educator started stringing together a beaded necklace. Another built a figure out of Legos. Several used the crayons to doodle on the table, drawing a picture or scribbling some notes. Others were hesitant, looking at the items and wondering what we might do with them, but never actually creating anything. There was something preventing them from diving in, some obstacles they needed to overcome. As adults, we are often hesitant about expressing our creativity, and so are our students.

Despite the opportunities presented, some learners are stuck in a creative struggle, unsure of what to do or where to start. Many wait for directions, not knowing if exploring with materials is encouraged or even allowed. We can design engaging spaces and create invitations to learn in new ways, but if we haven't created a culture that supports creativity, our students will remain stuck.

Let's equip them with strategies to respond to creative frustrations, so that when they are faced with obstacles in their learning, they can overcome them. From creative struggles, our students will learn to handle internal conflicts and recover from setbacks. By embracing creative struggles, learners will grow in new knowledge with the motivation to overcome barriers that occur throughout the journey.

I have two kids, both boys. They are active like many boys their age (five and seven), but I try to balance their physical activity with creativity. This can be tough at times. My mom tells me stories about how I would sit and color pictures when I was young, doodling on scratch paper or creating masterpieces in my coloring books. She claims I would entertain myself for hours, but moms of boys know that this is not usually in their nature.

When my boys were young, I started to build their creative stamina by doing "projects" and experimenting with creative materials. We explored with cardboard, painted pictures, and created with Play-Doh. I wanted to provide them with ways to be creative and foster the joy that I gained when I tapped into my creativity.

My older son Caden has a creative mind. He looks at materials and wonders what he can this it into? He was ecstatic when a new book arrived at our house, Epic Cardboard Adventures by Leslie Manlapig. This is an incredible, full-color book with cardboard creations like you've never seen. Needless to say, my son wanted to make EVERY-THING; Egyptian pyramids, royal crowns, time machines, and musical instruments. That afternoon, we made medieval swords and shields. It's amazing how duct tape and cardboard can fuel a little creativity genius.

Each project that we tried to tackle presented us with some challenges. My son got frustrated, but he never gave up. Somehow when the struggles started to sneak up on us, he just pushed through with an alternate plan or a new idea. "What if we tried this? Can we move it this way? I'm not sure if this will work, but if not, I have another idea." He was resilient in his creative thinking, never phased by a setback.

Why is it that our youngest learners rarely seem to face the creative struggle? They are naturally inquisitive. They are unconventional in their thinking. Their creative minds are forever processing new and imaginative ideas. Let's capture that same sense of enthusiasm and wonder and inject it into our classrooms!

ENCOUNTERING CONFLICT

As creative individuals, sometimes we just get stuck. That feeling of being stuck without a solution for getting unstuck can lead to internal conflict. When we are conflicted, the creative struggle may make us want to give in and give up. When we can't think of what to write next, we are tempted to crumple up the paper and throw it away. As we plan to design a solution for a challenge but encounter roadblock after road-block, we may throw up our hands in defeat. When the creative process is at a standstill, we frustratingly consider canceling the whole project. As adults, we do this sometimes and so do our students, but we don't have to let the creative struggle get us down.

The conflict that comes from our creative struggle can be a huge turning point for our students. It's the moment when we have to decide to dig in and persevere or succumb to the struggle. When our students encounter this, it can be emotional — even debilitating. We can support them, so they begin to see that conflict itself can be a good thing. It can bring awareness to the struggle, allowing students to recognize it and respond to it with flexibility and perseverance.

We can help equip our students with tools to bounce back from setbacks and overcome creative roadblocks in their way. The tools we provide will not only give them strategies for the classroom but also provide guidance for handling challenges outside of the school setting. As they increase their awareness, they can choose which strategies might work for them in each situation. The conflict will force them to reflect on their current progress and decide about where to go next.

STRUGGLES LEAD TO GROWTH

When you are in the midst of a creative struggle, it may seem like you'll never find your way out. It can feel lonely and even hopeless. It can be disappointing until you find a way to overcome the barriers. Once you push past the roadblock, the creative struggle can turn into a rebirth of creative energy. A creative struggle may lead you to a breakthrough and new learning.

This is when our students often grow the most. They have experienced some sort of creative setback, or maybe they've proclaimed that they'll never be creative, yet they have persevered and accomplished something remarkable. Whether faced with writer's block or grappling to find a solution to a problem, students will struggle with the creative process at times. The struggle may be internal but may also be interpersonal. Students may need your support as they build collaborative skills to fuel their creative development.

We have to remember to support them through the struggle, even when they doubt their capabilities, even if the outcome does not turn out exactly the way they planned. Not only can students grow in their academic and creative strengths, but their confidence will also grow when we support students through their creative struggle. Each time students encounter a struggle and successfully navigate that roadblock, they will increase their ability to handle other obstacles as well.

BOUNCE BACK

Our creativity is unlimited if we continue to fuel the spark. When we encounter setbacks and allow that spark to become dull, we risk the chance that the spark will fade away. We can be proactive in our creative journey and plan to bounce back from frustrations, to forge ahead in the face of a challenge.

Inevitably we will all face a creative struggle, reaching a point when we seem to be at a loss for new ideas. When this happens to our students, many of them will have a hard time bouncing back from this. We need to equip them with strategies to cope with the possible frustration that comes with the creative cycle of learning.

Even the most creative minds come to this crossroads where they've lost their sense of inspiration or just need a brain break to get rejuvenated. Sometimes a physical break might help students, boosting their creativity through some physical movement. Some students might benefit from a quiet moment to focus their thoughts and zero in on their creative process. We also need to equip students with the understanding, the language, and the confidence to persevere through a creative struggle in a productive way.

> IT IS WHAT WE DO IN RESPONSE TO THE FEELING OF STRUGGLE THAT WILL DETERMINE OUR FUTURE SUCCESS.

MODEL AND MENTOR

It is important for students to understand the creative struggle that they are experiencing is normal. We all go through this. Even experts encounter roadblocks on their creative journeys. As leaders of creative learning, we have a responsibility to be role models for our students. We can show them that the creative process isn't always easy and can offer our mentorship to students who are developing their personal creativity. Here are two ways we can model and mentor our students:

- Use a think-aloud strategy to demonstrate your thinking for students. As you are working in the classroom, voice your own learning obstacles or frustrations for your students. For example, "Writing is really hard for me. My ideas don't always flow like I want them to. Sometimes I need to take a breather before I return to my work." Acknowledging this struggle and talking about how we handle frustration as adults gives students the language for how they can respond to creative barriers. Students will understand that this is a "normal" feeling, that there are ways to bounce back and keep moving forward.

- Make your challenges public by sharing stories of your epic failures. For example, "I have such a hard time using this app. No matter what I do, I screw it up. Can someone show me what I'm doing wrong?" This vulnerability shows students we don't always know everything. When we show our failures, we are not only modeling what it feels like to be stuck, but we are also showing students how to ask for help when we need it.

Share your thoughts and your creative failures with your students, modeling your ability to embrace a creative struggle and move forward. Open up and share stories with the class that will demonstrate your ability to bounce back from and overcome obstacles in your learning.

GO WILD!

Ideas lost their flow? Creative sparks sputtering out? Sometimes you just need to let go. You know when your students need a brain break. You see that they're restless and having trouble focusing. Maybe they just need to go wild. What does this look like in the classroom?

For younger students:

- Try GoNoodle! https://www.gonoodle.com/ A little movement and dancing can give students the physical exertion they need to return to their work and keep the creative ideas going.
- Literally go wild! Call out an animal name and have students act like the animal, making sounds, movements, and behavior like that animal.

When students sit for extended periods, their minds begin to wander. We may feel this way at times, too. Learners can lose focus and may need a strategy to re-engage them in the learning. By adding in a little fun movement throughout the day, their focus can remain steady, and their creativity will flow.

For students at any level:

- Try some jumping jacks or other quick repetitive exercises to get the adrenaline going.
- Turn on some music and take a dance break. Let your students show off their best dance moves or just rock out for a minute or two. This kind of musical break will help to clear heads and refocus creative minds.

Implementing these physical strategies are crucial in helping students keep their creative minds moving. It also allows students to acknowledge they are having a creative conflict while equipping them with a strategy to effectively navigate the struggle. You'll be amazed at the students' ability to get back to work after a kinesthetic brain break. Not only will this get the blood flowing, but students may return to their task with a renewed sense of excitement and creative possibilities.

TAKE A MOMENT FOR MINDFULNESS

When you are faced with a mental block, how do you respond? Do you get frustrated and shut down? We know our students do at times. Do you step back, take a breath, and find a way to regroup? Do you have some "go-to" strategies that help you in times of creative struggle?

Taking a break from what you are working on can refresh your creative energy and allow you to refocus on your task. Mindfulness can help clear your mind of clutter and look at the task through a new lens. Sometimes that may seem hard to do within a classroom of 25 students, but there are small strategies that you can employ in the classroom (or within your personal life) that can provide a moment of clarity through your creative roadblock.

Moments of mindfulness can happen in different ways for different people. Mindfulness can come in the form of:

- Quiet meditation.
- Stretching or yoga.

- Listening to relaxing soundscapes.
- Laying down and practicing deep breathing.

Consider how you might make this work in your classroom. This time can be guided by you or even by a student. The mindfulness practices can be done with the whole class, in small groups, or as individuals. This type of brain break may not be for everyone, but it is an option your students might take advantage of to increase their creativity and focus in the classroom. Here's how a dose of mindfulness can work:

Step 1: Set aside three minutes. This could be a quick break in the midst of the craziness of the day, or the same time every single day. Once this has become a creative habit, consider extending the time to five minutes each day.

Step 2: Choose an activity from the bulleted list or design one on your own. For example, let's listen to a nature soundscape. Set a timer for three minutes and just relax and take in the sounds.

Step 3: As the time winds down, provide a verbal prompt letting students know when there are ten seconds left to ease them back into the learning. Focusing on processing the auditory input will allow you and your students to take a break from the learning and return to the task with a fresh perspective.

ASK FOR HELP

This strategy may sound really simple at first —ask for help. When you are experiencing a creative struggle, sometimes you just need to share it with someone. Expressing your frustration or telling someone about your struggle might just help you snap out of it. This can happen through conversations, but sometimes we aren't able to verbalize our struggle. Maybe we don't even want to admit the struggle to others, so we don't ask for help. In turn, we will need to develop other learner-centered strategies to work through a creative struggle.

Create a resource within the classroom students can access when they're facing a creative struggle. Here are two simple strategies you could make available in your classroom as a support for students who are in the midst of a creative struggle. These strategies can also work well for students who are having academic struggles.

- Support Jar: Create a basket, jar, or other type of container that can be a resource for students. Inside, students can place notes of creative encouragement or advice for peers to overcome the roadblock they are facing. The jar might include things like:
- You have creative potential!
- Try a different pathway to success.
- Take a break and then get back to work. You got this!
- You are doing a great job—keep it up!
- The ideas will come to you—don't give up now!
- Activate your creative juices.
- Help Desk: Any student who is out of ideas or needs some creative support can go to a designated location in the room for help. This can be a table or other spot that can facilitate small group conversations. When someone chooses to sit at the help desk, students or the teacher can sit and offer guidance or a listening ear for the person who is stuck.

As adults, when we are faced with a creative struggle, we tap into our individual coping skills and utilize personal strategies we think will be effective for the situation. Our students need to be equipped with strategies they can use to embrace the struggle and persevere in their creative journey. Asking for help is crucial for us to find ways to help every student, even the ones who refuse to ask.

BREAK DOWN ROADBLOCKS

As we take bold steps to unlock creativity in the classroom, we have to understand, there will be roadblocks. Our students will experience creative struggles that may or may not require our intervention. We can be proactive by developing strategies that will assist learners in overcoming their creative struggles and using resources within the classroom to break through those barriers. These are strategies that we can use as creative educators as well. Finding ways to take kinesthetic breaks, ask for help, and refocus through mindfulness practices are all options we can explore.

CREATIVE CONSIDERATIONS

Overcoming creative struggles can be frustrating, but we can provide strategies for our students to push past their creative barriers. How do you break through your own creative struggles? What structures can you put in place within your school or classroom build student capacity to embrace creative struggle both inside the classroom and out?

INVITATIONS TO IMAGINATION

Take a proactive step toward preparing your students to respond to feelings of creative struggle. Help equip them with the skills and strategies to tackle roadblocks and push through creative barriers.

• Add some mindfulness to your creative routine by adding stretching, reflection, or deep breathing.

• Design a classroom resource that can support and encourage learners through a creative struggle.

• Try a kinesthetic breakthrough movement or dance to get the creative juices flowing.

• What words of wisdom would you share with someone encountering a creative struggle? Tweet out a phrase of creative encouragement using #UnlockCreativity.

CELEBRATE CREATIVITY

 It is the supreme art of the teacher to awaken joy in creative expression and knowledge. — Albert Einstein

THE JOY OF LEARNING

Celebrations are joyful occasions in our lives where we lift up special people or events that impact our families and our lives. Birthday parties, weddings, or reunions—these are times when we gather together and connect around the joy of a special occasion. Often filled with conversations, smiles, and food, our celebrations represent an opportunity to honor the path of others.

Our personal and familial celebrations bring us immense joy and pride in the development and accomplishments of others. It is this same joy and pride that we need to bring into our schools to uplift the work of our students. This is especially true when it comes to creativity. We can unveil the joy of student learning in the way that we intentionally recognize creative thinking in our classrooms. The type and style of school celebrations will be different, just as it is with the special occasions in our personal lives. Sometimes the celebrations are huge events involving lots of people, while other times they are smaller, more intimate ways to honor accomplishments. Both types of recognition are important. Take the lead from your students on the kind of celebrations that will best meet their needs and interests.

You have come on this journey to open a world of creativity for your students. You have developed creativity in yourself and unlocked new opportunities for your students. By incorporating STEAM learning, a creative mindset for making, and the meaningful integration of technology, you have unlocked creative learning for students. As you have developed creative habits and tried to embed creative tasks in your classroom; you've increased the creative agility of your students in powerful ways, and now it is time to celebrate the learning.

As creativity is unlocked in the classroom, it is important to take time to celebrate the accomplishments of your students. When students take risks in the classroom, find a way to shine a light on their work. As groups of students collaborate on an entrepreneurial project or participate in an engineering and design challenge, acknowledge the hard work of the students, and honor their creative agility. Developing a creative mindset may take some work, so incorporating celebratory events at different checkpoints over the year will reinforce their creative accomplishments.

FOSTERING PRIDE

When students have the opportunity to share their work with an authentic audience, they feel a sense of pride. Students seek out feedback to improve their practice and develop innovative iterations of their projects. They persevere through creative struggles, which can result in amazing learning and creative growth.

Building up student pride is a part of our responsibility as teachers and school leaders. We need to seek out ways to celebrate the accomplishments of our students. We do this for athletics and academics, but we also need to recognize the creative growth and success of our students. Let's find those moments of pride to celebrate the creativity in our classrooms!

We must take time to recognize the accomplishments of our students, especially when extending themselves creatively might be out of their comfort zone. We can plan experiences that embed personal reflection, sharing, and celebration within our classrooms and also implement school-wide opportunities to share the creative work of our students. Recognizing accomplishments in creativity may look a little different from other areas. When we celebrate a creative mindset, we acknowledge the growth and development of our students throughout the creative process without focusing on the end product.

A SENSE OF COMMUNITY

When we come together to celebrate something, it often brings a group of people closer together. Relationships are built. Smiles are brightened. Bonds are strengthened. Hugs are shared. Think about the celebrations that are important to you; birthdays, anniversaries, family reunions, Sunday dinners, or neighborhood block parties. These are traditions that bring together those people that you care about most, your family and friends. You gather around for a happy occasion and honor special moments, creating a sense of togetherness with those that gather.

A sense of community is built, as you feel a common bond with those who are there to celebrate alongside you. The act of coming together presents an opportunity for you to connect with other people. It is a shared experience.

When we celebrate the creativity of our students, we are showing that we value their contributions and feel that they deserve to be recognized. The celebration expands to family, friends, and other community members as we invite those who are important to join in with us. Students will feel the love as the collective group celebrates their creativity.

WE CAN UNVEIL THE JOY OF STUDENT
LEARNING IN THE WAY THAT WE
RECOGNIZE CREATIVE THINKING IN
OUR CLASSROOMS.

CREATIVITY NOTEBOOK

If you have young children then I'm sure your refrigerator looks a lot like mine. It's covered with artwork, award certificates, and creative masterpieces in the making.

It's the place where we showcase the work of our children. It is the family version of a trophy case. We celebrate their ideas and their creativity by posting it in a public place and calling attention to their personal work.

My sons know that their creativity is valued. We have moved beyond the fridge to hang their paintings on the door to the back deck and a large picture window in the dining room. We have a collection of frames in the hallway that highlights creative work from different stages of their lives. They see these images every day. Images that they have created.

I always remind them that the colors they chose, the imagination they've expressed and the creativity they possess provides joy to others.

LIFT UP STUDENT LEARNING

When a team wins a game, they celebrate their victory. When a musical concludes, the group celebrates with an after-party. When students learn, how do we celebrate? Celebrating creativity in our schools is a way to publicly acknowledge the joy of student learning. It presents an opportunity to include school and community stakeholders in the celebration of creative learning. It is important to invite school leaders, teachers, parents, and community members to participate in this joyous celebration.

We can create opportunities to lift up the creative work of our students. This can happen through small gestures or large exhibitions of creativity. Take a creative approach to your celebration. Try to find unique ways to acknowledge student creativity in the classroom. These can be generated with your students, giving them a voice in the process.

If creative learning is important, then we need to treat it that way. When we celebrate the creative growth our students experience, we show them these skills are valued. We can honor the work of our students in ways that will heighten their creative work and share it with others.

CREATIVITY COFFEE HOUSE

Picture a casual boutique coffee house where regulars gather for a drink and positive vibes - not the national chain on every corner, but the neighborhood shop where you're handed a ceramic mug and given a welcoming smile. This is the place where friends gather to chat and share a drink. It smells delicious. It feels cozy. How might we create this environment in our classroom?

Transform your classroom into a neighborhood coffee house and create a casual vibe to support creative student accomplishments. Can you picture it? Dim the lights in favor of some lamps. Play some light music in the background. Everyone can bring in a mug from home and indulge in some tea or hot chocolate. Students can take turns "taking the stage" and sharing a poem, a creative breakthrough, or a project idea. Let's broaden the celebration!

What can we do?

- Invite parents and family to see a showcase of student work.
- Create handmade invitations to the "coffee house" celebration.
- Offer coffee, tea, and cookies.
- Visitors can enjoy creative presentations, displays of students' work, or demonstrations of creative skills.

The coffee house approach sets a different tone for creative learning. It conveys the message that creativity is valued and requires special attention. This strategy also expands the reach of creative thinking by including parents, families, and the community.

Another version of this type of sharing event can happen through "studio time." In a studio, you can see works of creativity in progress as artists work on projects. Picture a dance studio where ballerinas are stretching and practicing their routines. Consider a pottery studio where artists are working on projects and exploring with new materials. Open your classroom up to others during "studio time" so that observers can get a glimpse of the creative work happening in your space.

Within your classroom "studio" designate a place to spotlight work that exemplifies creativity.

What might this look like?

- Mount picture frames of different shapes and sizes on the wall that can display a variety of student work.
- Creative examples that don't fit into a frame can be showcased on podiums or display cases.
- Create a bulletin board entitled "Our Creative Collection" (or another creative name) and allow students to nominate the creative work of their peers to be displayed on the board on a rotating basis.

MAKE ROOM FOR REFLECTION

Students are inundated with information all day. They are busy reading, writing, and problem-solving in every classroom. You can imagine how full their brains must be with all that we are trying to stuff in there every day? If we want our students' creative juices to flow, we need to allow time for reflection. We are working to develop a creative mindset, and that requires time and space to look for the possibilities around them. Let's be intentional about setting aside time to just pause and reflect.

As we slow down and pause, we create time to reflect on accomplishments, both personal and collective. It is time to say, "Look at how you've grown in your creativity." Reflecting on student work and sharing feelings about the creative journey celebrates learning and development over time. It is often when we have the chance to look at our own collection of work and analyze how far we've come, that we can truly celebrate.

Time is a hot commodity in our schools with pressure to get through the curriculum, and even more pressure to perform on standardized tests. Perhaps you have to move at a certain speed through a district pacing guide. There are tests and meetings and schedules and assemblies. We never have enough time to get to everything, so making time for thoughtful reflection may fall by the wayside. Don't let that happen!

Wondering, thinking, and reflecting are an important part of the learning process, and we can't forget to embed them into our instruction time. Not only will this time provide you and your students with some much needed "downtime," but it can provide clarity, focus, and even the creative spark that we may be searching for. Are we intentional about giving our students time to absorb new information? What might that look like in the classroom?

Here are a few ideas about classroom reflection that support a creative mindset:

Wonder Wall

- Create a space in the room (a blank wall, bulletin board, or even a piece of chart paper) where students can post things they are wondering about—curious questions, research topics, passion project ideas. You could certainly make this digital using Padlet or another digital tool, but there is some value in maintaining an ongoing, visible spot in the room for this type of sharing. Don't forget to set guidelines for when and how students can post to the Wonder Wall.

Mindset Moments

- Set aside time for students to reflect on their creative mindset for making. These might be a-ha moments when students are cognizant of their mindset towards learning. Encourage students to jot something down on a sticky note or write ideas on a classroom whiteboard that demonstrate a creative mindset:
- "I used to be bad at drawing, but since I've tried sketchnotes I feel more creative in class!"
- "I never felt creative before until I tried . . ."
- "At first, I wasn't sure about working with my design team, but we are making a lot of progress with our project."
- "Today, I learned how to _____, and it has boosted my creativity!"

Recognizing a shift in mindset, taking time to exhale about our wonderings, and reflecting on our creative development can serve as celebratory steps in our journey. Reflection can be done in private through journaling or sketching, but creating public ways to share our reflections can be a way for all students to think more deeply about their thinking. When focused on creativity, reflection gives learners an insight into the perspectives and mindsets of others, which can encourage and support their own creative process.

CREATIVE COLLECTIONS

One way to celebrate the creative growth of your students over time is to develop a creative collection. Think about student portfolios, but with a focus on creativity of your students. This collection can be based on one class or course throughout the school year, or even an ongoing collection that could follow a student throughout their education. As you develop intentionality regarding the creative thinking in your classroom, you will begin to see a change in student interactions and in their work. How can we capture that creative growth over time?

The creative collection can be student-driven with each student determining the evidence they want to collect that demonstrates their creativity. These might be physical artifacts like something they've made in class. It could also include personal reflections about their journey to increase their creative agility. The collection might include videos or photographs documenting their creative successes and failures. It can serve as a celebration of their creative learning over time. The collection is not meant to be evaluative, but rather a way to gather some of the creative expression that you have fostered in your classroom.

Think about how a creative collection will support student voice as they reflect on their work and determine which pieces of evidence are important to them. Consider how student choice will come into play as they select the creative examples they want to represent their creative journey. The idea of a creative collection can be simple, a folder or file housing the student's creative artifacts. This strategy could also be paired with a larger celebration, combining the creative collection with the coffee house or studio time celebration.

A CELEBRATION OF CREATIVE LEARNING

Now that we have designed opportunities for students to express their creativity, it is time to celebrate. Celebrating student creativity can happen in small personal ways or in larger, more public events. We can call attention to the creative growth of students by writing them a note to praise their creative mindset. Sometimes a bigger celebration can be planned. Let your students decide how to honor the creative work of the class. This is the chance to celebrate creative learning in the way that works best for you and your students.

CREATIVE CONSIDERATIONS

Celebrating the creative accomplishments of your students will validate their work and bring attention to their creative talents. From small types of recognition to larger showcases of student work, think about the ways you might shine a light on student creativity. Is there a way to designate time and space to let others know that creativity is being fostered in your space? How does your school honor creative thinking? How will you show students that creativity is valued in your school?

INVITATIONS TO IMAGINATION

Embrace the opportunity to convey the importance of creative thinking in the classroom. Honor student growth in ways that will lift up creative learning.

• Write three personal notes of praise to recognize creative thinkers in your classroom.

• Transform your learning space into a cool coffee house and give students the stage to share their learning.

• Celebrate student work through open studio time, building in opportunities to discuss creative work and share ideas with others.

• Celebrate student creativity by sharing their work on social media. Take pictures during your creative celebration and share it on social media using #UnlockCreativity.

FINAL THOUGHTS

 Creative living is living a life that is driven more strongly by curiosity than by fear. — Elizabeth Gilbert

YOUR CREATIVE LIFESTYLE

As a child, he loved drawing. This love of art and imagery turned into a passion as he developed his artistic skills over time. He grew in his knowledge of animation and even tried to open his own theater, with little success. The need to express himself creatively continued to be a driving force throughout his life. Never letting that early passion fade, Walt Disney continued to be driven by his personal creativity and arguably developed one of the most imaginative places on earth.

Think about all that Walt Disney has created. Not just the theme parks and the movie studio that carries his name, although those are certainly part of the experience. Disney has built a lifestyle brand for people that lures them into creativity and imagination. His empire provides us with opportunities to notice small details and revel in grand gestures. The company has designed experiences that engage all of the senses through vivid images, awe-inspiring music, and interactive enjoyment.

With the shifts that have occurred in education over the last twenty years, now is the time to unlock creativity and embrace a creative lifestyle. As we look to the future, society will need problem solvers, collaborators, and creative thinkers who have the agility and stamina to excel in the global economy. In the past, we may have limited creativity in the classroom because it is messy or because it doesn't seem easy to implement. We might have limited it within our school systems because we feared the outcome or were too concerned that creative experiences were outside of our comfort zone, but now is the time to unleash creative opportunities for our students.

In order to embrace a creative lifestyle and develop our creative potential, much like Disney did, there are keys we can use to unlock and amplify our creativity in schools. Creativity is whimsical and unexpected at times. It can be challenging and joyful all at once. When you unlock creativity in yourself, you will notice ways to bring out the creativity in others. Revealing moments of creativity will happen when you use these seven keys to open your imagination and take in the creative opportunities around you.

SEVEN KEYS TO UNLOCK CREATIVITY

There are steps we can all take to build our creativity and the creativity of our students. The seven keys represent some of the ways we can embrace a creative lifestyle and build our creative stamina as individuals and as educators:

1. Develop creative habits.
2. Notice the small things.
3. Make time for playful exploration.
4. Champion the creativity of others.
5. Build your creative crew.
6. Celebrate creative successes.
7. Believe in yourself.

KEY #1 DEVELOP CREATIVE HABITS

Some say it takes twenty-eight days to make something a habit. With consistency and daily attention, the habit becomes part of what you do from that point forward. It may come naturally, or it may require more focused attention to make new habits stick. Walt Disney made drawing a habit, sketching daily, and trying new techniques. Developing creative habits can start with your first step.

Start simply with one habit that you want to embed into your creative lifestyle. Set an initial goal of one week. "This week, I am going to take a two-minute mindfulness break at the end of every day." The quiet time and reflection will help you feel refreshed and may even spark an idea for a creative lesson. Adding new habits to your repertoire will allow you to build up your creative agility, gaining new skills and strategies to incorporate creative thinking into your classroom instruction.

KEY #2 NOTICE THE SMALL THINGS

When we take time to notice the things around us, we are tapping into our five senses. With heightened awareness, we take an interest in the detailed patterns in local architecture, the sounds heard on the playground, and the vibrant colors of a flower garden. Disney wanted people to notice the creativity that went into the smallest details of his work through light, color, and mood. Noticing the everyday things helps us to build an appreciation for things around us, but also helps us develop an eye for creative expression in our midst. Noticing the design of a room or the curve of a smile, our attention to the small things can build our creative mindset. When we take it a step further and share our noticings with others, we are nurturing their curiosity and providing creative potential for them.

KEY #3 MAKE TIME FOR PLAYFUL EXPLORATION

Finding time to play is another step towards unlocking creativity. Playful exploration is an informal way to try new materials and explore new techniques. Be intentional about carving out time to tinker in this way. The act of being playful is what Disney was all about. The exploration of images, sounds, and movement can spark student creativity and inspire new ideas. Offer a variety of learning materials in the classroom. Ensure the flexibility of student collaboration through play. Expose students to unconventional items that can lead to discussion around possible inventions. Devote time to exploring alongside your students at every age and level so they can see you as a creative role model.

KEY #4 TAKE CREATIVE RISKS

Unlocking creativity may require you to step out of your comfort zone and into unfamiliar territory. Taking creative risks or trying something new will allow for personal and professional growth for you as an educator as well as creative growth for your students. Disney took bold steps throughout his creative journey pushing the limits of his own imagination and that of those around him. Without these innovative steps forward, it is likely he would not have experienced the success he did. Don't fear the failure that may come with each risk. Try it and know that you are taking a chance that may lead to unleashing the imagination of your students. Creative risks may be as simple as introducing a new assessment option to your students or as complex as creating a school-wide exhibition of creative learning. When we value student creativity, we have to be willing to take a risk to bring those opportunities to our students.

KEY #5 BUILD YOUR CREATIVE CREW

Walt Disney surrounded himself with creative individuals who could move creative ideas forward. Disney "Imagineers" envision new possibilities, share unthinkable opportunities, and engage in creative collaboration. It is through the collaboration with others that new ideas are planted, and tremendous opportunity grows.

Surround yourself with artistic individuals, creative thinkers, and imaginative problem solvers. Bringing people into your network who can help you on your creative journey, those who will help you and the students that you serve. When you are part of a creative crew, you benefit from the passion and knowledge of those around you. Build your crew by connecting on social media and through face-to-face experiences. Foster the relationships that will develop and sustain your creativity in the classroom.

KEY #6 CELEBRATE CREATIVE SUCCESSES

We celebrate the things we value. Family, special occasions, and notable accomplishments are celebrated in all aspects of our lives. We cherish these celebrations and make them special for all involved. Imagination is celebrated daily at Disney parks as everyone gathers for a parade or looks in awe at the incredible display of fireworks. This marvel of light, sound, and colorful imagery is a daily affirmation of the creative world Disney embodies. Creativity in our schools should be no different. If we want to recognize the growth and development of our students, we need to celebrate their creative successes.

Creativity can be hard work. Take time to celebrate successes, big and small. When you accomplish a creative goal, celebrate it. As students take creative strides, lift up their success with a celebration. You can celebrate with a kind word or a note of encouragement. You can also celebrate creative successes in larger ways that will promote creativity throughout your school community with public exhibitions, shows, and recognitions. Celebrate creativity by displaying student work that emphasizes student growth and development. When we lift up its importance, we are serving as champions for creativity.

KEY #7 BELIEVE IN YOURSELF

We started this book by beginning with the belief that we are all creative. It is that belief we need to instill in our students. Belief that we can all build our creative agility is key to achieving this goal. Believe that you can be creative, even if you've been told in the past that you weren't. Think about the creative habits you are working to develop and affirm that you are continuing to devote time and energy to getting better. Push aside feelings of doubt and continue to forge ahead, giving yourself permission to try and try again. When we demonstrate unshakable confidence and belief in ourselves, we demonstrate that positive energy to our students, building in them the belief that they can do anything, too.

Disney believed early on that he would use his skills to create something amazing. Through perseverance and continued belief in his ideas, Disney built a creative empire that immerses children and families all over the world in wonderful imagination and creative possibility.

Using these seven keys will allow you to unlock creativity in the classroom and open a world of imagination for your students. Each key in itself will support you on this creative journey, but when many keys are unlocked together, you can unleash the creative potential within your classroom.

NOW, MORE THAN EVER, IT IS TIME TO UNLOCK CREATIVE OPPORTUNITIES FOR OUR STUDENTS.

THE POWER OF CREATIVITY

The goal of this book was to inspire you to unlock creativity and open a world of learning for your students. We've shared small ways to infuse creativity in the classroom through tasks like the 30 Circle Challenge or taking a mindfulness break to refocus and re-energize our creative juices. We've engaged creativity in bigger ways through designing new systems and experiences and developing empathy towards others. Hopefully, you have been able to grab onto a few ideas that you can use to boost your own creativity but more importantly, ideas that you can implement with your students to #UnlockCreativity.

CREATIVE CONSIDERATIONS

We can use our powers to empower agile, creative thinkers. We can help equip them with the skills and dispositions needed to solve complex problems and express themselves in extraordinary ways. You are ready to boost student creativity. You can start by making a commitment for the next seven days to complete one creative task. The #UnlockCreativity community will be there to support you. While there are a lot of different ideas within the book for you to try, here's one connected opportunity you might be ready to take. If you still feel like you need some direction and the support of creative colleagues around the globe, we have an opportunity for you!

Need more guided support as you tiptoe into developing creative habits? Join in the 7 Day Creativity Challenge! We can all commit to trying something for just seven days, right?

7 DAYS OF CREATIVITY FOR EDUCATORS

Here's how it works:

- Plan to participate in all seven days of the challenge. Set a reminder on your phone or on your calendar, so you don't forget.
- Complete the challenge of the day.
- Post a picture on social media sharing your creativity with others.
- Don't forget to include #UnlockCreativity.
- Once you've completed all seven days, it's time to celebrate!
- Send me a message saying that you've completed the challenge

—I'd love to feature your creativity on my website or in a future blog post.

TAKE THE 7-DAY CREATIVITY CHALLENGE

Day 1: Write a five-word definition of what creativity means to you.
Day 2: Take a picture of an unusual image that will start a creative conversation and post it on social media.
Day 3: Write down three creative topics that you would like to learn about.
Day 4: Go to the dollar store with $7 and make something with the items you buy.
Day 5: Write a note to someone only using pictures.
Day 6: Come up with seven uses for a milk carton.
Day 7: Take a selfie doing something creative and share it on social media.

Join the #UnlockCreativity Community so you can join in additional rounds of the creativity challenge throughout the school year. Be on the lookout for new and different creative tasks for future challenges.

BONUS – COMMIT TO CREATIVITY

They say it can take 28 days to create a habit, so let's see if we can extend our creativity into the classroom with this commitment to creativity. Here's a 20-day challenge that you can do with your students. Each day incorporate one creative task in the classroom. Some tasks are more complex, and while others are quick and simple. Take photos of your students in action, post examples of their work, and share with the #UnlockCreativity community on social media. View the challenge details on the next page.

20 Day Creativity Challenge				
Write one creative goal for yourself.	**Create a sketchnote for one of your classes.**	**Paint a self-portrait.**	**Take a 10-minute mindfulness break.**	**Redesign your bedroom.**
What do you need to ensure you will reach this goal?	How do drawing and sketching impact your learning?	What does your portrait let others know about who you are?	What types of mindfulness practices work best for you?	What features are important to you and why?
Watch a TED Talk on creativity.	**Design a logo for your class (or a club or group that you're involved in).**	**Build a structure with Legos.**	**Make a handmade greeting card and send it to a friend.**	**Build a space rover that could land on Mars.**
What did the speaker share that provides new insight into this topic?	What creative tools helped you to create your logo?	How do different building materials help or hinder your learning?	How did you infuse creativity into your design?	What materials did you use and why?
Write a poem with just 12 words.	**Make a mask—connect it to a story, a culture, or time period.**	**Create a robot that will have specialized skills to meet your needs.**	**Write a 30-word story.**	**Take a photo of an interesting plant or animal.**
Why did you choose the topic that you did?	Describe the connection that you chose and why.	What skills does your design include and why?	What challenges did you encounter with the limits placed on this challenge?	What intrigued you about this creature?
Create a playlist of songs that boost your creativity.	**Write a thank-you note to someone who inspires you to create.**	**Design a chair for the classroom.**	**Create a class song or chant.**	**Draw the last place you traveled to.**
What made you choose these songs? What features do they have in common?	Why does this person inspire you?	What unique materials do you plan to use?	How will you share your song or chant with others?	Where did you travel and why?

30 CIRCLE CHALLENGE

REFERENCES

EdCamp Foundation. (n.d.). Retrieved from https://www.edcamp.org/

Gonzalez, J. (2016). How pineapple charts revolutionize professional development. Retrieved from https://www.cultofpedagogy.com/pineapple-charts/

Kaplinsky, R. (2016) #ObserveMe. Retrieved from https://robertkaplinsky.com/observeme/

Kim, K. (2011). The creativity crisis: The decrease in creative thinking scores on the Torrance Tests of Creative Thinking, *Creativity Research Journal, 23*(4), 285-295.

Maslyk, J. (2018). 3 word design challenges. Retrieved from https://jaciemaslyk.blogspot.com/2018/01/3-word-design-challenges.html

Martinez, S. L., & Stager, G. (2013). *Invent to learn: Making, tinkering, and engineering in the classroom.*

ABOUT THE AUTHOR

An educator for the last 22 years, Dr. Jacie Maslyk has served as a classroom teacher, reading specialist, elementary principal, and assistant superintendent. She has a Bachelor's Degree in Elementary Education from Indiana University of Pennsylvania (IUP) and a Master's Degree in Instructional Leadership from Robert Morris University. Her doctorate was earned in curriculum and instruction, also from IUP.

Jacie has published numerous articles on topics like principal leadership, designing effective interventions, and leading STEAM and Making in schools. She is the author of *STEAM Makers: Fostering Creativity and Innovation in the Elementary Classroom, Connect to Lead: Power Up Your Learning Network to Move Your School Forward* and *Remake Literacy: Innovative Instructional Strategies for Maker Learning.* Jacie is a featured blogger with Demco, Defined STEM, and Education Closet, as well as maintaining her own blog, *Creativity in the Making* at www.jaciemaslyk.blogspot.com.

Maslyk is a member of a variety of educational organizations including for The Association for Supervision and Curriculum Development (ASCD), The International Literacy Association (ILA), and The American Association of School Administrators (AASA). She is also a long-time member of the Pennsylvania Principals Association and was awarded the Frank S. Manchester Award for Excellence in Journalism in 2015 by the organization. She was also a National Distinguished Principal (NDP) finalist in Pennsylvania in 2013 and 2014. She has presented throughout the United States and Canada on topics ranging from leadership and literacy to creativity and maker education. Jacie also serves as an educational consultant providing professional development and coaching to teachers and school leaders. Connect with Jacie on Twitter @DrJacieMaslyk or email her at jaciemaslyk@gmail.com.

OTHER EDUMATCH TITLES

EduMatch Snapshot in Education (2016)
In this collaborative project, twenty educators located throughout the United States share educational strategies that have worked well for them, both with students and in their professional practice.

The #EduMatch Teacher's Recipe Guide
Editors: Tammy Neil & Sarah Thomas
Dive in as fourteen international educators share their recipes for success, both literally and metaphorically!

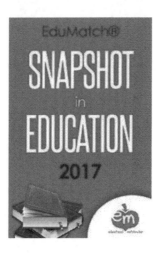

EduMatch Snapshot in Education (2017)
We're back! EduMatch proudly presents Snapshot in Education (2017). In this two-volume collection, 32 educators and one student share their tips for the classroom and professional practice.

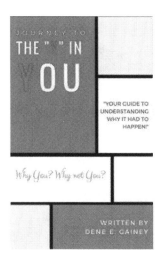

Journey to The "Y" in You by Dene Gainey
This book started as a series of separate writing pieces that were eventually woven together to form a fabric called The Y in You. The question is, "What's the 'why' in you?"

The Teacher's Journey by Brian Costello
Follow the Teacher's Journey with Brian as he weaves together the stories of seven incredible educators. Each step encourages educators at any level to reflect, grow, and connect.

The Fire Within
Compiled and edited by Mandy Froehlich
Adversity itself is not what defines us. It is how we react to that adversity and the choices we make that creates who we are and how we will persevere.

EduMagic by Sam Fecich
This book challenges the thought that "teaching" begins only after certification and college graduation. Instead, it describes how students in teacher preparation programs have value to offer their future colleagues, even as they are learning to be teachers!

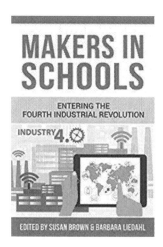

Makers in Schools
Editors: Susan Brown & Barbara Liedahl
The maker mindset sets the stage for the Fourth Industrial Revolution,
empowering educators to guide their students.

Divergent EDU by Mandy Froehlich
The concept of being innovative can be made to sound so simple. But what if the
development of the innovative thinking isn't the only roadblock?

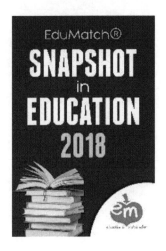

EduMatch Snapshot in Education (2018)
EduMatch® is back for our third annual Snapshot in Education. Dive in as 21
educators share a snapshot of what they learned, what they did, and how they
grew in 2018.

Daddy's Favorites by Elissa Joy
Illustrated by Dionne Victoria
Five-year-old Jill wants to be the center of everyone's world. But, her most
favorite person in the world, without fail, is her Daddy. But Daddy has to be
Daddy, and most times that means he has to be there when everyone needs him,
especially when her brother Danny needs him.

Level Up Leadership by Brian Kulak
Gaming has captivated its players for generations and cemented itself as a fundamental part of our culture. In order to reach the end of the game, they all need to level up.

DigCit Kids edited by Marialice Curran & Curran Dee
This book is a compilation of stories, starting with our own mother and son story, and shares examples from both parents and educators on how they embed digital citizenship at home and in the classroom.

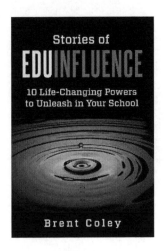

Stories of EduInfluence by Brent Coley
In Stories of EduInfluence, veteran educator Brent Coley shares stories from more than two decades in the classroom and front office.

The Edupreneur by Dr. Will
The Edupreneur is a 2019 documentary film that takes you on a journey into the successes and challenges of some of the most recognized names in K-12 education consulting.

In Other Words by Rachelle Dene Poth
In Other Words is a book full of inspirational and thought-provoking quotes that have pushed the author's thinking and inspired her.

To Whom it May Concern
Editors: Sarah-Jane Thomas, PhD & Nicol R. Howard, PhD
In *To Whom it May Concern...*, you will read a collaboration between two Master's in Education classes at two universities on opposite coasts of the United States.

One Drop of Kindness by Jeff Kubiak
This children's book, along with each of you, will change our world as
we know it. It only takes *One Drop of Kindness to fill a heart with love.*

Differentiated Instruction in the Teaching Profession by Kristen Koppers
Differentiated Instruction in the Teaching Profession is an innovative way to
use critical thinking skills to create strategies to help all students
succeed. This book is for educators of all levels who want to take the
next step into differentiating their instruction.

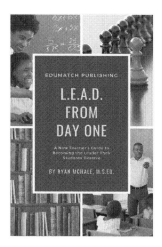

L.E.A.D. from Day One by Ryan McHale

L.E.A.D. from Day One is a go-to resource to help educators outline a future plan toward becoming a teacher leader. The purpose of this book is to help you see just how easily you can transform your entire mindset to become the leader your students need you to be. So what are you waiting for? The time is now.

educational matchmaker

Made in the USA
San Bernardino, CA
14 July 2020

75524554R00120